# Mapping
## the News

## Case Studies in GIS and Journalism

*David Herzog*

ESRI PRESS
REDLANDS, CALIFORNIA

ESRI

Mapping the News: Case Studies in GIS and Journalism
ISBN 1-58948-072-4

First printing May 2003.

Printed in the United States of America.

*Library of Congress Cataloging-in-Publication Data*
Herzog, David, 1963-
Mapping the news : case studies in GIS and journalism / David Herzog.
    p. cm.
    ISBN 1-58948-072-4 (pbk. : alk. paper)
    1. Journalism—Computer network resources. 2. Geographic information systems. I. Title.
    PN4729.3.H47 2003
    070.4'0285—dc21                                        2003009536

Published by ESRI, 380 New York Street, Redlands, California 92373-8100.

Books from ESRI Press are available to resellers worldwide through Independent Publishers Group (IPG). For information on volume discounts, or to place an order, call IPG at 1-800-888-4741 in the United States, or at 312-337-0747 outside the United States.

# Contents

# *Preface*

Computer-assisted reporting has been one of the most significant developments in U.S. journalism during the past two decades. Print and broadcast journalists have added depth to routine stories and helped lay the foundation for investigations by analyzing data with software tools: primarily spreadsheets and database managers.

In recent years, a growing number of journalists have added geographic information systems (also called GIS) to their toolkits and now can dig deeper into data and visualize otherwise unnoticed geographic patterns. Other professions have used GIS for much longer, but journalists are starting to catch up.

Journalists have used GIS for plenty of great stories since the landmark year of 1992, when the *Miami Herald* used GIS to uncover the damage patterns left by Hurricane Andrew. I wrote this book because I wanted to showcase some of that great work in one volume.

The introduction of this book provides a primer on GIS and how journalists can use it. The case studies that follow show how journalists at newspapers across the country used GIS in their reporting and include step-by-step examples that illustrate key GIS functions. Two appendixes offer pointers for getting started with GIS and finding free data.

This book is meant for all kinds of journalists: the newsroom managers who want to know more about the power of GIS; the journalists who like reading the inside stories of how other journalists used GIS analysis; and student journalists looking for inspiration.

*David Herzog*
*February 2003*

# *Acknowledgments*

*Mapping the News: Case Studies in GIS and Journalism,* like so many books, has one author and a big supporting cast. The influence of so many people is all over the pages of this book and I would like to thank some of them here.

First, thanks go to the fellow journalists who helped and inspired me when I was initially trying to figure out how to use computer tools to analyze data for news stories. John Freed, then of the *New York Times,* opened my eyes to the power of GIS in news reporting with his presentation at the first Computer-Assisted Reporting Conference in 1993. Also, thanks go to Steve Doig, who helped the *Miami Herald* win the Pulitzer Prize in 1993 with his GIS work and has since helped spread the gospel among journalists.

Second, thanks go to the editors who supported my interest in using GIS with training, time, and resources: David M. Erdman at the *Morning Call,* in Allentown, Pennsylvania, and Tom Heslin at the *Providence Journal.*

I'd also like to thank R. Dean Mills and Brian Brooks at the University of Missouri School of Journalism for their longstanding support of computer-assisted reporting. Brant Houston, executive director of Investigative Reporters and Editors and the National Institute for Computer-Assisted Reporting, provided support and advice as I wrote this book.

Rachel Schaff, an Honors College student at the University of Missouri, assisted with research and helped secure permission for many of the graphics in this book. Carolyn Edds, director of the IRE Resource Center, and her staff also assisted with research.

Thanks go to David Boyles, my editor at ESRI Press, whose suggestions and gentle prodding helped make this a much better book. Also, thanks to everyone else who helped make this book happen: production designer Jennifer Galloway, copy editor Tiffany Wilkerson, and cover designer Denise Marshall. My thanks also go to Christian Harder and R. W. Greene at ESRI Press, and ESRI President Jack Dangermond.

Last, I want to thank two other people whose assistance was key in getting this book published: J. T. "Tom" Johnson, professor of journalism at San Francisco State University, and Kris Goodfellow, manager of business development for Internet Solutions at ESRI.

# Mapping the News

# *Introduction*

Every budding journalist learns to cover the news by asking some basic questions: Who? What? Where? When? Why? How? The answers to these questions provide much of the raw material for news stories.

Over the last decade some enterprising journalists in newsrooms across the United States have been using a new reporting tool—geographic information systems (GIS)—to dig deeper as they try to uncover exactly where the news is happening. Many media marketing departments have been using GIS to map demographics and the locations of viewers or subscribers; newspaper circulation departments have been using the programs to map the most efficient vehicle delivery routes. In newsrooms, however, the use of GIS is just getting a foothold.

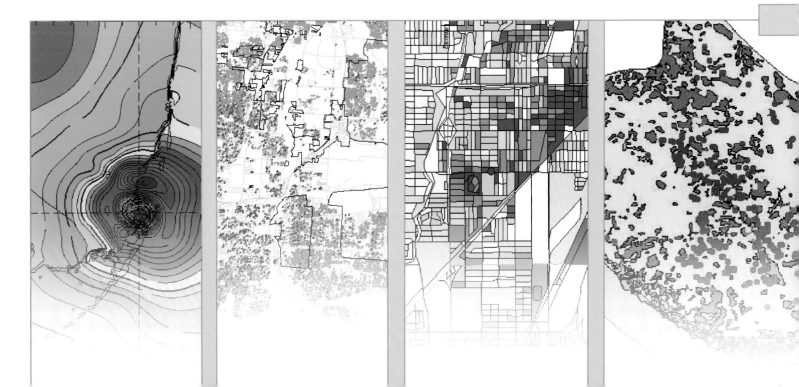

### Variety of uses

Since 1992, when reporters at the *Miami Herald* newspaper used GIS to plot the path of Hurricane Andrew over a surveying map and discovered that shoddy construction and lax inspections exposed thousands of houses to risk, journalists have turned to GIS to help tell a multitude of stories, as the case studies in this book will show. As you'll see, journalists have used GIS to map election results and display demographic information about neighborhoods with high rates of disqualified ballots. They have used GIS to pinpoint the locations of environmental hazards and identify neighborhoods with high rates of lead poisoning. Reporters also have used GIS to help paint portraits of demographic change during the 1990s. In fact, the primary catalyst for GIS in the newsroom is the U.S. decennial census. Journalists in only a few large newsrooms began using GIS during the early 1990s so they could make sense of data from the 1990 Census. Now, more journalists are using GIS to report on the data from the 2000 Census.

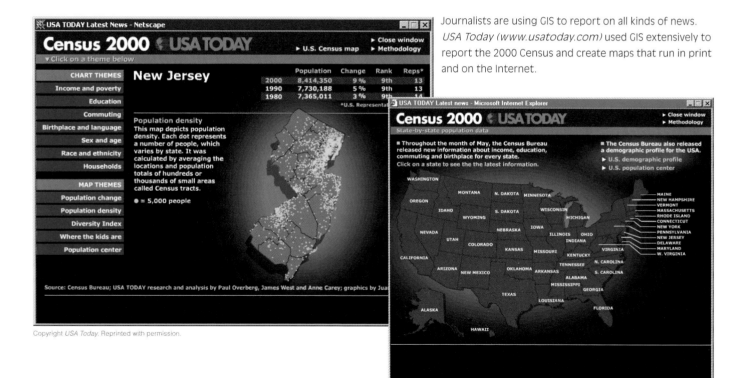

Journalists are using GIS to report on all kinds of news. *USA Today (www.usatoday.com)* used GIS extensively to report the 2000 Census and create maps that run in print and on the Internet.

## An integrated system

Broadly defined, a geographic information system is a system of hardware and software used for the storage, retrieval, mapping, and analysis of geographic data. So a journalist who wants to do GIS work needs three things: the hardware (a computer, monitor, maybe a plotter to create large maps); the GIS software itself, along with any add-on programs that allow more sophisticated analysis; and geographic data (files that display maps on the computer monitor).

Many other professions have extensive histories of using GIS. Transportation planners use GIS to untangle highway snarls, geologists use mapping to explore for oil, and telecommunications planners use GIS to build and maintain networks. Police agencies now use GIS to look for "hot spots" of particular crimes, while emergency management agencies in cities, states, and the federal government have deployed GIS since September 11, 2001, to simulate terrorist attacks on U.S. soil and craft response plans.

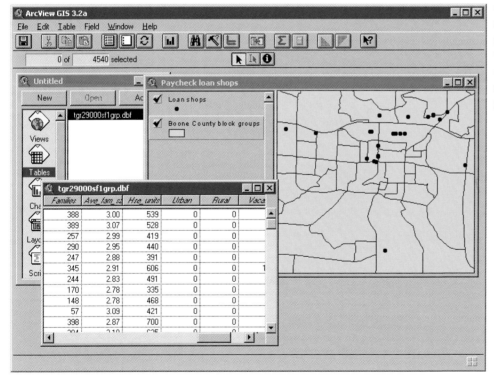

GIS programs, such as ArcView® software, developed by ESRI, integrate and display geographic data, maps, and tables. In this example, the software is used to plot business locations on a map, and also show a data table relating to specific geographic areas called block groups.

## Beyond just maps

Print and broadcast journalists for decades have employed maps to display information and communicate with readers or viewers. We've all seen maps, created by graphic artists, showing where something happened: the plane crash, a double murder, an earthquake overseas. We've also seen color maps, relying on census data, that show how similar geographic areas compare to each other in terms of population, income, race, or education level.

GIS allows journalists on the beat or working on exhaustive investigations to take mapping to a higher level. They can map government data or tables of data they create themselves, and then look for patterns. Journalists can use GIS to select data. They can find geographic elements that are near each other. For example, a journalist can use GIS to identify schools that are close to environmental hazards.

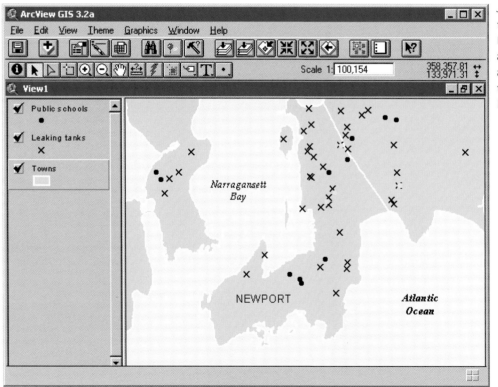

Journalists use GIS to find geographic features that are close to each other. In this example, ESRI® ArcView displays as yellow dots the public schools in and around Newport, Rhode Island, that are within five hundred feet of a leaking underground storage tank.

## Slow but steady progress

Why now? Why are journalists starting to adopt GIS as a reporting tool? There are several reasons.

First is the continuing evolution of computer-assisted reporting, the analysis of databases compiled by government agencies. Thousands of journalists across the country have learned how to use spreadsheets, database managers, and statistical programs to squeeze interesting and relevant stories out of government data. Organizations such as the National Institute for Computer-Assisted Reporting (NICAR), based at the University of Missouri, offer GIS training tailored for journalists.

Second is the evolution of GIS itself. Once largely the domain of mainframes and powerful network servers, GIS can now be used on desktop computers that are capable of storing more data than ever and processing it at even quicker speeds.

The National Institute for Computer-Assisted Reporting (NICAR), based at the University of Missouri in Columbia, trains journalists how to use GIS to uncover news stories. The Web address is *www.nicar.org*.

A third reason for the emergence of GIS in journalism is the deployment of GIS in government agencies. From city hall to the state house to federal government departments, GIS use is spreading. Many of these agencies provide the data at no cost, though some charge fees. The fourth reason is the wide availability of GIS data on the Internet. All over the Web—on government agency, university, and commercial sites—anyone can download GIS data at no cost. In many states, GIS consortiums run Web sites that serve as clearinghouses for the publicly available data. For example, the Rhode Island Geographic Information System (RIGIS) makes more than a hundred mapping files available for free download to users who register and accept a licensing agreement. As all these forces converge, journalists themselves are taking their maps and their data and posting it on the Web so readers and viewers can interact with the information.

Boulder County, Colorado, is one of many government agencies that rely on GIS to deliver key services. Journalists can often obtain geographic data from these agencies free or at low cost.

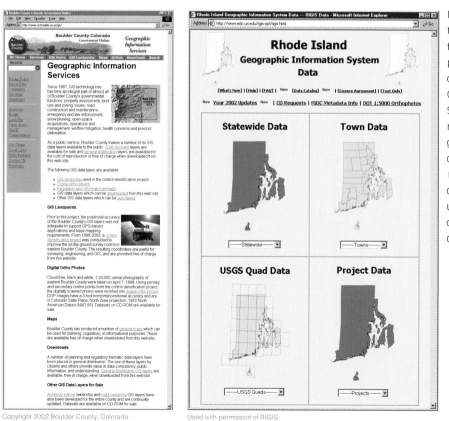

Copyright 2002 Boulder County, Colorado.

Used with permission of RIGIS.

Many states are making their geographic data files available to the public on the Web. Users of the Rhode Island Geographic Information System (RIGIS) can find more than a hundred geographic data files on the consortium's Web site at *www.edc.uri.edu/rigis*. By clicking various topics, the user can see detailed lists of files available under the different categories.

## Basic terms and elements

Before you look at some of the best uses of GIS to make the news, it's helpful to become familiar with how the programs work. Here are some of the major concepts:

- Journalists using GIS software work with two types of data: *geographic* and *attribute.* The geographic files display map *features,* or geographic items. Those items can be natural, such as a river, or man-made, such as a bank branch location. Attribute data is stored in a table that contains information about a geographic element. An example: home mortgage loan rejection rates by census tract.

- Geographic files contain data and attached shapes: polygons, lines, or points. Polygons represent areas, such as city neighborhoods. Lines are used to represent rivers, roads, and railways. Points can be used to show the location of cities, wells, and crime scene locations. ArcView geographic files are called shapefiles, layers, or coverages.

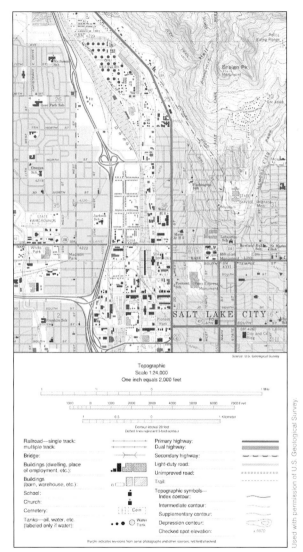

Journalists can use ArcView to examine attribute data, such as this table of home mortgage loan application results in Arizona compiled by the federal government. Each record is supposed to specify the census tract of the property used to secure the loan, so journalists can easily map this data.

Geographic features can be natural or man-made. This topographic map of Salt Lake City, Utah, shows both types in great detail.

- GIS programs share common functions: *layering* map features on top of each other; *selecting* records to find geographic features that meet criteria specified by the user; *joining* tables so the user can attach data to geography; *geocoding* to take street addresses stored in data tables and create pin maps; and *symbolizing* data to display differences in data values between geographic areas.

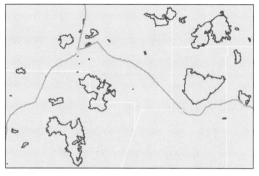

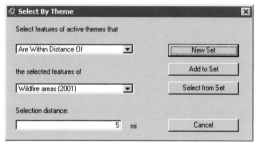

With the Select by Theme function, journalists can find features in two different themes that are near each other. Here, Select by Theme is used to identify northern Nevada cities within five miles of a wildfire in 2001. ArcView displays the selected cities as yellow stars.

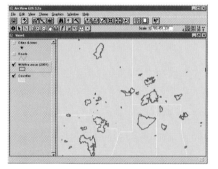

GIS programs work by layering map themes (related geographic information, such as rivers, roads, city or county boundaries) on top of each other. This example of a northern Nevada wildfire map was created by opening the county map (top left) and then adding the wildfire areas (top right), roads (lower left), and cities (lower right).

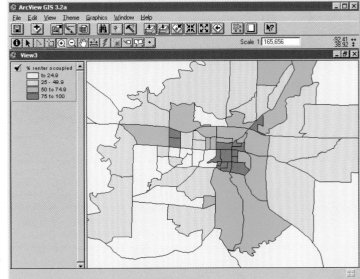

During geocoding, the GIS program attempts to create points for addresses stored in an attribute table. ArcView software's geocoding editor function lets the user manually select the correct address from the table attached to a streets file.

ArcView can symbolize data in many ways. Here, it uses a color theme map to display the percentage of housing units occupied by renters inside census block groups in the city of Columbia, Missouri. Increasingly darker shades of green indicate increasingly higher percentages of renters living within specific census block groups.

### Case studies and GIS

The case studies that follow will show how journalists use the powers of GIS to uncover great stories and do groundbreaking reporting. Many of the journalists using GIS today to bolster their reporting depend on software produced by ESRI, the world's largest company fully dedicated to GIS.

The next chapter starts with a blockbuster story, the first major use of GIS in investigative reporting.

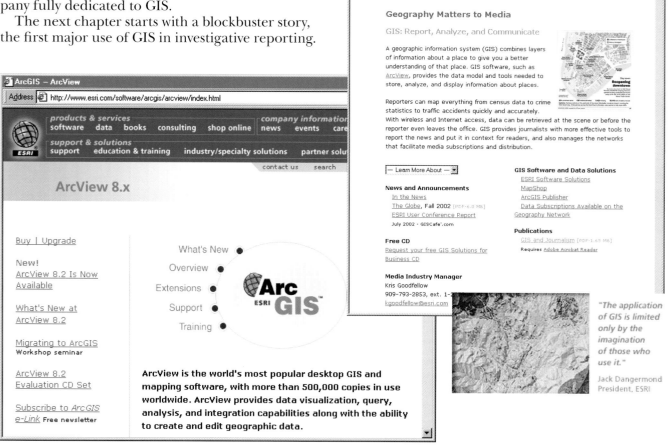

From ESRI's Web site at *www.esri.com,* users can navigate to *www.esri.com/media* and learn how GIS software can help journalists in a multitude of ways. A link to the ArcView pages lets users learn more about how the software works.

## Acknowledgments

Barbara Maxwell
Director and Permissions Officer, *USA Today* Library
For Web graphics reprint permission.

Gina L. Bramucci
For Columbia, Missouri, payday loan shop data.

Brant Houston
Executive Director, Investigative Reporters and Editors, Inc., and the National
Institute for Computer-Assisted Reporting
For Web graphic reprint permission.

Amanda Hargis
GIS Coordinator, Boulder County, Colorado
For Web graphic reprint permission.

John Stachelhaus
Coordinator, Rhode Island Geographic Information System
For Web graphic reprint permission.

# 1 *Decoding a hurricane's destruction*

South Florida sits right in the middle of "Hurricane Alley" and has been battered by some of the strongest tropical cyclones of the twentieth century. Bordered by the Atlantic Ocean on the east and the Gulf of Mexico on the west, the millions of people who live on the peninsula lie vulnerable to the most violent hurricanes in the United States.

In August 1992, Hurricane Andrew—with winds topping 130 mph—blazed a path of destruction through the housing developments of Dade County, to the south of Miami. Though the city largely had been spared this category 4 storm (ranked on a scale from 1 to 5, with 5 being the most severe) homes in suburban subdivisions suffered extensive damage. No hurricane in the previous eight decades matched Andrew in terms of financial loss. All told, Andrew caused nearly $35 billion in damage, according to estimates by the federal government based on construction costs in the year 2000.

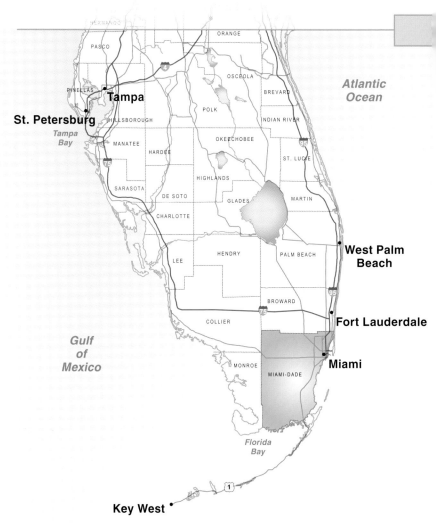

## Reporters get busy

Soon after the hurricane struck, reporters at the *Miami Herald* newspaper started covering the massive recovery effort. Around the same time, owners whose homes had been battered and flattened began questioning how the damage could be so severe. After all, the conventional wisdom at that time held that south Florida had the toughest building code in the country. Some homebuilders said the devastation was an "act of God," and that the homes could not have been built to withstand the extreme winds.

A team of reporters, led by the newspaper's investigations editor, was summoned to answer the question: Was the extent of the damage indeed an "act of God," or were there any shortcomings caused by builders, inspectors, or government officials that put the homes at risk? GIS would play a key role in answering that question, and help launch a new avenue of inquiry for journalists.

## Using GIS

One of the reporters on the team, a database specialist, had experience using computers and tables of government information, such as real estate assessment rolls, to research news stories. Shortly before the hurricane, he had been using a Macintosh®-based program to map demographic patterns in data from the 1990 Census. He believed that mapping could answer some of the key questions the newspaper was asking about the damage caused by Hurricane Andrew.

Early in the news-gathering effort, another member of the reporting team learned that the local Red Cross had been compiling a database of storm damage. The reporter obtained a copy, but it turned out to be unusable because it largely contained unstructured notes, rather than the structured database tables, arrayed in columns and rows, that GIS programs use. Later, the same reporter learned that Dade County was surveying the damage itself in a more methodical manner, and entering its findings into a structured database.

The Florida peninsula lies dangerously exposed to hurricanes. Millions of people live here, in what Floridians call "Hurricane Alley."

Used with permission of National Aeronautics and Space Administration (NASA).

## Investigating information

The *Herald* database specialist quickly obtained a copy of the county's database, even though it had information about just eight thousand—or 10 percent—of the damaged homes. The database contained a record for each property. Each record included the unique property identification number assigned by the county and whether the home was habitable.

Because the database contained the unique property ID, it could be joined to the county's property assessments database that the *Herald* already had in-house and updated annually. That database contained a wealth of data about the properties: year built, value, subdivision. Also, inside the property ID there was a string of characters that identified the township, range, and section in which the property was located. Each unique township, range, and section is a one-square-mile unit that is used in land surveying.

The reporter lacked a subdivision map layer for his new mapping program, Atlas GIS™ for PC, so he decided to build a map file from scratch. Rather than build a subdivision layer, which would have been too time-consuming, he built a layer that displayed each township, range, and section.

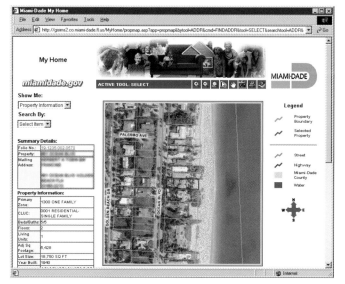

A *Miami Herald* reporter merged a damaged-homes database with tax assessor records for his analysis. The Miami–Dade County government Web site *(miamidade.gov)* has links to various kinds of property information. (Dade County became Miami–Dade County a few years after Hurricane Andrew struck.)

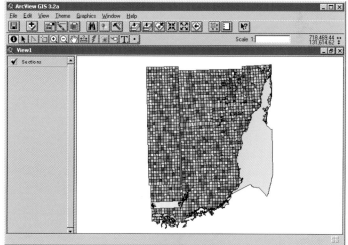

Each unique township/range/section unit covers one square mile. The *Miami Herald's* reporter created a similar grid covering a smaller area of Dade County in his GIS program for the mapping analysis.

The reporter could have created the layer by drawing polygons in his mapping program, but he opted for an automated method to create the layer. He used a Microsoft® Excel spreadsheet to automatically generate a text file that defined the geographic coordinates for each unique section and then opened that in Atlas GIS.

The *Herald* needed one more map layer file before it could start its analysis: a wind contour showing the speed of the hurricane winds by area and air pressure. A local hurricane researcher provided that on paper and the *Herald's* reporter drew the lines of the contour in Atlas GIS to create the new layer.

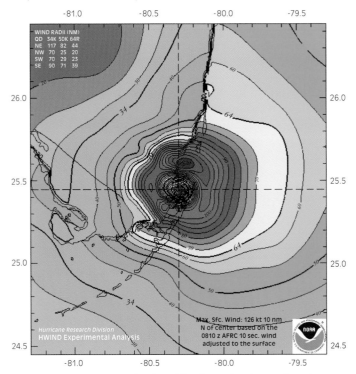

## Hurricane Andrew 0900 UTC 24 Aug. 1992

*Max. 1-min sustained surface winds (kt)*
Analysis based on aircraft data adj. to the surface from 700 mb and surface wind reports

This wind speed contour developed by the National Oceanic and Atmospheric Administration (NOAA) shows the intensity of the winds from Hurricane Andrew. The *Miami Herald's* reporter obtained a similar grid on paper and reconstructed it in his GIS program.

## Identifying variables

Before he launched into the final stages of analysis, the reporter identified the variables that he thought might have an effect on the percent of inspected homes declared uninhabitable in each square-mile section. First he wanted to check the obvious: whether the areas closest to the highest winds suffered the most damage. So he created a thematic map with a unique color displaying the percentage range of homes damaged in each section and laid the wind contour layer over that. That revealed no clear pattern; some of the sections several miles from the center of the storm had high damage rates, as high as 90 to 100 percent. After mapping a few other factors that revealed no clear patterns, the *Herald's* database reporter struck gold.

He mapped the damage by the year each home or structure was built. The map clearly showed that areas with newer homes were more likely to have high rates of destruction. As Dade County inspectors entered more damage report information into their database, the *Herald's* reporter obtained the fresh data and repeated his mapping again and again to test whether the damage patterns remained consistent. They did. Eventually, the *Herald* had data about more than sixty thousand damage inspection reports and an explosive story that ran in a special section that December.

The *Miami Herald* published its findings in a special section than ran four months after Hurricane Andrew struck. The special section contained a rich array of maps and photos documenting the damage patterns.

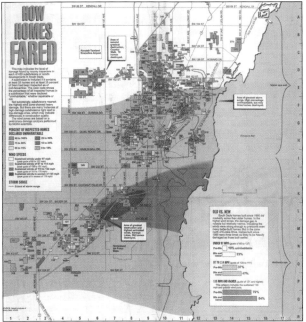

Used with permission of the *Miami Herald*.

This map, which ran in the *Herald*, shows the percent of inspected homes declared uninhabitable by subdivision. Some areas several miles from the center of the hurricane suffered greater damage than some of the areas adjacent to the center. Though not a GIS-produced image, it's an example of how the *Herald* enhanced its coverage with effective mapping.

17

## Investigative findings

The *Herald's* investigation found that homes built since 1980 by some of the county's biggest developers were rife with design and construction flaws. Homes in one of the most devastated subdivisions lacked proper roof bracing. In other homes, roofs failed because builders used staples instead of nails—an effort to save money. Additionally, the newspaper reported that building inspectors could not keep up with the construction boom; they had been inspecting four times the number of homes that could be done properly. Some inspection reports had been fabricated, the *Herald* found. In addition, the reporters found that in the previous five years, inspectors on 194 occasions were assigned to do fifty or more inspections in one day. A grand jury just two years earlier had recommended a limit of twenty inspections a day by each inspector.

The GIS analysis helped the *Herald* identify adjacent south Florida neighborhoods with widely differing damage levels. Reporters then visited those neighborhoods and photographers went to take pictures. The *Herald's* database specialist also used Atlas GIS to create a series of four maps printed on the back cover of the sixteen-page section that illustrated the force of the storm and the damage it left behind.

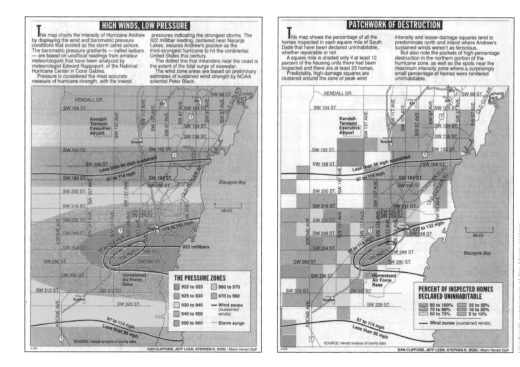

The *Herald's* reporting team used GIS to help develop maps that ran in the paper's special report. The map on the left uses color variations to show relative barometric pressure and how it related to hurricane damage. The map on the right shows percentages of inspected homes declared uninhabitable, whether repairable or not.

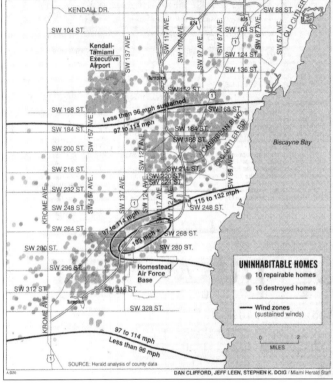

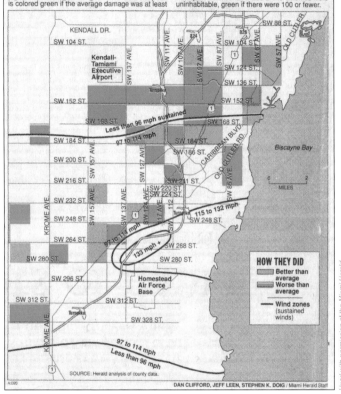

## UNINHABITABLE HOMES

This dot-density map indicates the number and approximate location of nearly 15,000 homes south of Kendall Drive declared "uninhabitable" by county inspectors in the weeks following Andrew.

The blue dots represent uninhabitable homes that were deemed "repairable." The red dots represent homes damaged so badly that they need to be demolished.

Notice the dot patterns in relationship to the wind zones on the map. For instance, in the area around the worst wind zone, the oval just north of Homestead Air Force Base, there is a heavy pattern of destruction, as would be expected.

But there also is heavy damage in the zone north of SW 168th St., an area where hurricane scientists believe the sustained winds stayed below 96 mph., well below the maximum winds specified in the South Florida Building Code.

**UNINHABITABLE HOMES**
- 10 repairable homes
- 10 destroyed homes
— Wind zones (sustained winds)

0    MILES    2

SOURCE: Herald analysis of county data.

DAN CLIFFORD, JEFF LEEN, STEPHEN K. DOIG / Miami Herald Staff

## SOME BETTER, SOME WORSE

If homes built since 1980 were constructed like those built earlier, the average level of damage for both should be approximately the same. What this map shows is where homes built since 1980 were damaged to a significantly greater or lesser extent than those nearby.

A square is colored red if the average damage to homes built since 1980 was at least 50 percent higher than average damage to all homes. A square is colored green if the average damage was at least 50 percent less than the average.

For instance, if there are a thousand homes in a specific square mile — including 400 built since 1980 — and half of all homes were uninhabitable, then 200 built since 1980 should be uninhabitable. This map shows only those square miles where the damage difference is at least 50 percent greater or 50 percent less. The square in this example would be red if 300 or more homes were uninhabitable, green if there were 100 or fewer.

**HOW THEY DID**
- Better than average
- Worse than average
— Wind zones (sustained winds)

0    MILES    2

SOURCE: Herald analysis of county data.

DAN CLIFFORD, JEFF LEEN, STEPHEN K. DOIG / Miami Herald Staff

The dot-density map on the left displays the locations of repairable homes and destroyed homes. The map on the right shows where homes built since 1980 were damaged to a significantly greater or lesser extent than those nearby. Taken together, the maps on this page and the previous page helped show areas where severe damage would not have been expected, and they helped to buttress the paper's reporting on shoddy building and inspection practices.

### Major findings

GIS helped the *Herald* to show that, without a doubt, the devastation pattern was no "act of God," but the result of shoddy construction and lax regulation. After months of debate, officials in Dade County and neighboring Broward County in 1994 toughened the south Florida building code. Under the new rules, contractors had to use more nails to attach plywood sheets to roof rafters. In addition, builders had to install stronger doors, windows, and shutters on their new homes.

The *Herald's* investigation of the slipshod construction and inadequate inspections helped the newspaper win journalism's highest honor—the Pulitzer Prize—and sparked interest in using GIS to analyze data for stories. Other journalists saw that GIS could be a powerful reporting tool.

The *Herald* won a Pulitzer Prize in 1993 for its coverage of the hurricane recovery effort. GIS played a large role in the newspaper's coverage.

## Acknowledgments

Steve Doig
Knight Chair in Journalism, Cronkite School of Journalism and Mass Communication,
Arizona State University, and formerly of the *Miami Herald*
For providing information about the use of GIS in reporting on Hurricane Andrew,
and for providing a reprint of the 1992 special newspaper section that detailed the
findings of the *Miami Herald* investigation.

Hiram Henriquez
The *Miami Herald,* Graphics Editor
For newspaper graphics reprint permission.

Lissette Elguezabal
The *Miami Herald,* Photography Sales Manager
For newspaper graphics reprint permission.

Judi Zito
Miami–Dade County government
For Web graphics reprint permission.

Sig Gissler
Administrator, Pulitzer Prizes
For Web graphics reprint permission.

1

# $2$ *Tracking demographic changes*

Every ten years the federal government attempts to count every person living in the United States, and gather information about their race, gender, age, ethnicity, and household. The decennial census—mandated by the U.S. Constitution for the purpose of apportioning seats in the U.S. House of Representatives—is a massive undertaking. And it produces gigabytes of no-cost data containing information about people, and how they work and live.

Researchers of all kinds use the U.S. Census Bureau data to look at the demographic characteristics of areas as large as the nation as a whole and as small as a city block. By mapping census data, demographers can identify census tracts with high concentrations of elderly residents. Market researchers can find neighborhoods whose residents mirror a target customer profile. Governments can focus social services by mapping and identifying high rates of child poverty. Journalists can use the census data as a rich tip sheet for stories, provided they are able to sift through mountains of data stored in tables. In Southern California's San Diego County, a reporter at the *Union-Tribune* newspaper did that and found compelling stories with GIS.

## Examining change

At the *San Diego Union-Tribune*, the reporter assigned to analyze the Census 2000 data for San Diego County knew that the area had changed during the 1990s. Its population had grown and become more diverse. The reporter also knew that if he used GIS to map tract level data he could see exactly how the population of neighborhoods had changed since 1990. Census tracts in urban areas often mirror neighborhood boundaries.

Census 2000 generated a wealth of data that's being used by journalists across the country. The Census 2000 Web site is at *www.census.gov/main/www/cen2000.html.*

## Legwork begins

Preparing to analyze the data took weeks. Before the Census Bureau even released the first big batch of data from the 2000 Census, the reporter started gathering data and maps from the 1990 Census. He downloaded TIGER® maps from the Census Bureau Web site and converted them into shapefiles using TGR2SHP, a utility sold by GIS Tools, of Knoxville, Tennessee. The Census Bureau produces the TIGER files for its own mapping system, and the files need to be converted by the user before they can be opened in ArcView. The preliminary TIGER map files for 2000 had been released already, so he downloaded those too and converted them using the TGR2SHP utility.

Next he downloaded 1990 Census block-level data from the Associated Press Census 2000 Web site, a subscription service available to the wire service's members. He then processed the data contained in dBASE® tables and added the data to ArcView as tables. (dBASE is a database management system.)

The reporter used TGR2SHP, a program that can run by itself or as an ArcView extension, to convert the TIGER files from the Census Bureau into shapefiles. The program allows the user to select any or all TIGER layers for conversion.

The U.S. Census Bureau makes its TIGER mapping files available for free download on the Web. The TIGER files are located at *www.census.gov/ geo/www/tiger*. TIGER is an acronym for Topologically Integrated Geographic Encoding and Referencing system.

TIGER files are designed to run in the Census Bureau's electronic mapping system. Users need to convert these files—which contain a series of text instructions for drawing map features—into shapefiles before using them in ArcView.

### Coordinating information

When the Census Bureau in March 2001 released the data that was collected from everyone who was counted, the reporter downloaded it from the Associated Press Web site and got to work. But there was a hitch: the reporter couldn't simply compare changes among census tracts for 1990 and 2000 because the Census Bureau had changed the boundaries of many of these geographic areas for the 2000 Census.

So he needed a tool that would allow him to fit the 1990 blocks and data into the 2000 tract boundaries. He used Two Theme Analyst, an ArcView extension that many journalists are using, available for free at the ESRI Web site. Extensions are programs that expand the capabilities of ArcView and can be accessed through the View menu at File\Extensions in ArcView 3.x. In ArcView 8.x, the extensions can be accessed in the ArcMap™ application menu at Tools\Extensions. Extensions that are written by ArcView users are posted on ESRI's ArcScripts Web site *(arcscripts.esri.com)* and are available for free download. ESRI and other companies also sell extensions—ArcView 3D Analyst™ is an example—that they have developed.

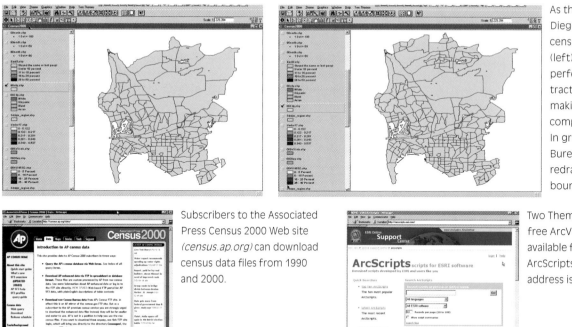

As these two views of San Diego County show, the census tracts for 1990 (left) do not correspond perfectly to the census tracts for 2000 (right), making tract-to-tract comparisons impossible. In growing areas, Census Bureau officials often redraw census tract boundaries.

Subscribers to the Associated Press Census 2000 Web site *(census.ap.org)* can download census data files from 1990 and 2000.

Two Theme Analyst and other free ArcView extensions are available for download at ESRI's ArcScripts Web page. The address is *arcscripts.esri.com.*

## Using the extension

Two Theme Analyst takes the data from a source polygon theme and allocates it to a target polygon theme based on the percentage of source theme that overlaps the target theme. For example, if a 1990 Census block group (the source) is completely within a 2000 Census tract (the target), Two Theme Analyst assigns 100 percent of the population to that tract. However, if 25 percent of a 1990 block group overlays one 2000 tract and 75 percent of another 2000 tract, it will divide the numbers accordingly: 25 percent of the block group population will be assigned to the first tract and the remaining 75 percent to the second tract. Two Theme Analyst takes the computed values and stores them in new fields in the target table.

After the reporter ran Two Theme Analyst to process the data, he opened the data table for the 2000 tracts and in a database manager program created a new field for the population change between 1990 and 2000. Next, the reporter created a thematic map that showed the population change in San Diego County. In the Legend Editor, he selected graduated colors—shades of red in this case—to show the population gains. While the county as a whole grew by nearly 13 percent during the 1990s, the map showed clearly that the growth was uneven. The south county suburbs boomed while some seaside communities lost population. A three-column map on the front page of the paper showed readers the patterns.

Using the same data, the reporter used ArcView to show the population trends differently for another color map that ran inside the newspaper. This time he used the Legend Editor to create a dot-density map that showed the distribution of population growth within the census tracts. Each dot represented one hundred people who were added to the population of the census tracts.

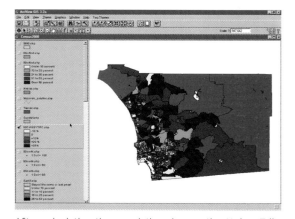

After calculating the population change, the *Union-Tribune's* reporter mapped it by census tract in ArcView. Darker shades indicate areas with greater population increases. This GIS map later became the basis for a front-page map that ran in the newspaper and showed population change at the neighborhood level in some areas of San Diego County.

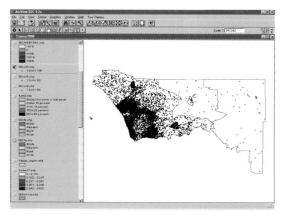

The reporter looked at the change another way: by creating a dot-density map (based on the same data) that displayed every one hundred additional people as a dot.

### Shifting gears

After giving its readers the essential news about growth, the newspaper in the days that followed turned to reporting on diversity, a major issue in Southern California. The wave of diversity that had swept through the Los Angeles region and other parts of California had hit San Diego County in a big way during the 1990s. In fact, from its initial reporting, the *Union-Tribune* knew that in the 1990s the Hispanic population had grown 47 percent countywide, faster than the 13 percent growth overall in the county. As part of its efforts to uncover pockets of diversity, the newspaper wanted to map the minority population growth and see where ethnic minorities had become the dominant population groups.

Measuring diversity turned out to be simple. As part of its census data package, the Associated Press calculated and provided a diversity index score for the geographic areas as a field in the data tables. That way, journalists could see by tract, place, or county just how diverse an area was. The scale, developed by *USA Today*, measures the likelihood that two people picked from random within an area would be of a different race.

The *San Diego Union-Tribune's* March 30, 2001, edition carried major coverage of Census 2000 and what the impacts were for San Diego County.

Reprinted courtesy of the *San Diego Union-Tribune.*

The Associated Press calculated a score in its data tables that showed diversity in each geographic area. That score, based on a formula developed by *USA Today,* measured the likelihood that two people picked at random from the geographic area would be of a different race.

## Seeing via maps

The reporter mapped the diversity scores by tract, because the newspaper wanted to see what was happening in the neighborhoods. The results were clear: the areas along the Pacific Ocean coastline remained white and lacked diversity. In the inland areas to the south and the east, the mapping showed, the neighborhoods with established minority neighborhoods saw an increase of their minority populations during the 1990s. Narrowing in on the city of San Diego, the reporter's GIS analysis showed that the most diverse neighborhoods were primarily in the southeastern part of the city. After the mapping found that City Heights was the most diverse neighborhood in the city—and the county—another reporter visited a Vietnamese market there and saw an African American resident shopping at the meat counter. She interviewed the shopper and used that telling scene to begin her story.

The newspaper ran a map of San Diego city that highlighted its most diverse neighborhoods. The diverse tracts were shaded with four colors to indicate which group—white, black, Latino, or Asian—had the greatest population within each. It showed that areas that already were diverse had become even more diverse during the 1990s.

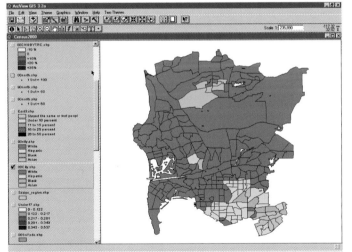

The *Union-Tribune's* reporter created a map that showed which racial group (white, black, Hispanic, or Asian) had the highest population in each tract. This map zeros in on the city of San Diego and shows the dominant populations: whites (dark brown areas); blacks (olive green); Hispanics (yellow); and Asians (tan).

The *Union-Tribune's* April 6, 2001, edition explained how City Heights had the most racial diversity of any place in the county. The map that appeared in the paper was developed in part by the effective understanding and use of GIS.

### Investigating home ownership

The *Union-Tribune* wondered whether the Hispanic population gains had translated into Hispanic home ownership gains. The reporter covering the Census wanted to use GIS to map out the Hispanic ownership rates across the county. He knew that, thanks to skyrocketing prices for homes, housing remained out of reach for many Hispanics.

The home ownership rate in San Diego County—at 55 percent in 2000—was significantly less than the U.S. rate of just under 67 percent. For Hispanics, the county rate was even lower at around 40 percent. Clearly Hispanics lagged. This time the reporter mapped the data by ZIP Code, because he also wanted to analyze median home-sales prices reported to the ZIP Code level that the newspaper had purchased from a private vendor.

After mapping the home ownership rates, the reporter could see that the Hispanic home ownership rates were highest in established Hispanic neighborhoods. In other areas, the mapping showed, Hispanic homeowners had made slower inroads. The home sales data from the private vendor showed that the ZIP Codes with the highest rates of Hispanic home ownership also had some of the county's least expensive housing.

Many other newspapers continue to map census data to look for stories. A few newspapers have mapped the population data by race to document the rise of segregation and, in some cases, show how certain cities have become more integrated.

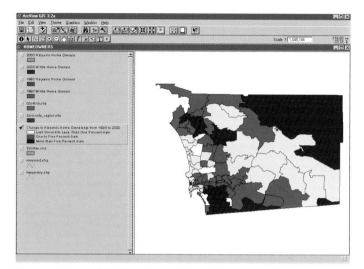

The reporter used ArcView to map Hispanic home ownership change during the 1990s at the ZIP Code level and compare that to median sales prices. This map's light pink areas show regions where home ownership of Hispanics either lost ground or made gains of less than 1 percent. The red areas show gains of 1 to 5 percent, and the darker brown areas show gains of more than 5 percent

The *Union-Tribune* effectively used mapping in its April 7, 2001, edition to explain how increasing numbers of Hispanics were buying homes in San Diego County.

Reprinted courtesy of the *San Diego Union-Tribune.*

## Acknowledgments

David Washburn
Investigative Reporter, the *San Diego Union-Tribune*
For providing information about the use of GIS in reporting on Census 2000, program screen shots, and newspaper articles.

Brian Craigin
Deputy Graphics Editor, the *San Diego Union-Tribune*
For providing permission to reprint newspaper article scans.

Mark Cardwell
Executive Producer, AP Digital
For providing permission to reprint the Associated Press Census Web site home page.

# 3 *Seeing schools in black and white*

Education news is a staple of every newspaper. Parents want to know whether their children are getting a quality education, and they want to be assured their kids are safe in school. Property owners want to know about school budgets and whether their tax bills will rise. In the Charlotte–Mecklenburg, North Carolina, public schools, parents had something else to think about: the busing of students to achieve racial integration.

For more than three decades, busing had been a hot-button issue. In a 1971 landmark decision, the U.S. Supreme Court upheld the busing of Charlotte–Mecklenburg students as a way to desegregate schools unconstitutionally divided along color lines. By the mid-1980s, busing had lost some of its public support. That eroded even further during the 1990s as newcomers unaccustomed to busing flooded Mecklenburg County and raised the population 36 percent. In 1997, a Charlotte–Mecklenburg parent sued the school district in federal court, contending that the school system had become integrated and busing was no longer needed. Several other parents later signed onto the suit as plaintiffs and asked the court to order an end to the district's race-based school assignment policies. That set the stage for a journalistic inquiry that relied in part on GIS.

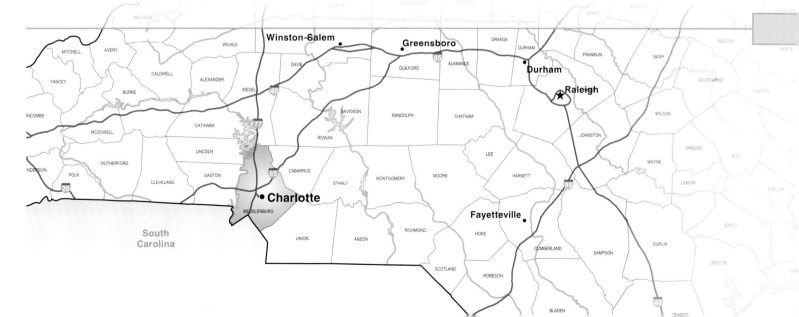

## Acquiring information

Reporters at the *Charlotte Observer* had been watching the case develop and were curious about a simple question: What would happen to more than ninety thousand students if a federal judge ordered the district to dismantle its system of busing and assign students to neighborhood schools? GIS provided the answers that in turn laid the foundation for a five-part series that ran in the newspaper during January 1999, before a judge had even ruled upon the parents' suit.

One of the *Observer's* reporters had been negotiating with school district administrators, attempting to get a file from the district's GIS system that showed the residences of ninety-four thousand students for the 1997–1998 school year. The school administrators also kept data about each student's name, race, gender, grade level, school attended, and home address. The reporter had used GIS regularly since the early 1990s—when he reported the results of the 1990 Census for the *Observer*—and knew that he could measure the effect of busing African American and white children to school if he had the file.

After three or four months of discussion, the reporter and school administrators compromised: the administration agreed to release the data, minus the students' names and exact home addresses. Instead, district officials created a point for each student that approximated the true home address. The district provided the data as an ESRI ArcInfo™ export file that the reporter opened in Atlas GIS, his mapping program. The school district also provided a point file that displayed the locations of all the schools in the district.

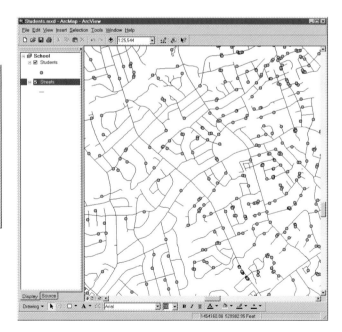

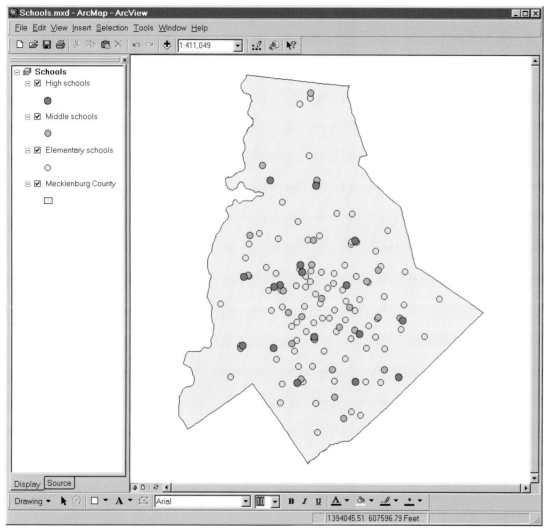

The *Observer* obtained an ArcView shapefile from the school district that contained a record for each student (table, previous page) and included points that marked their approximate home address locations (map, previous page). The school district also provided a shapefile with the locations of all the public schools (above).

## Analyzing the data

For each student record in the database, the reporter used Atlas GIS to calculate information that would be essential to the stories: First, he performed a function in Atlas GIS that calculated the nearest appropriate school (elementary, middle, or high school) for each student and automatically entered the school identification numbers in a new field. Second, he calculated the straight-line distance that each child actually traveled to school, and the distance that the child would have to travel if the student attended the closest appropriate school. Also, the reporter calculated a poverty weight for each student, based on the child poverty percentage in the surrounding census block group.

That analysis yielded some powerful findings for the series: nearly half of the students were bused past their nearest school. Almost twenty-eight thousand students—most of them African American—were bused to desegregate or because the nearest schools were packed. Another twenty thousand children took the bus to magnet schools, which offer specialized programs and attract students from across the district.

| SUMLEV | STATEFP | CNTY | TRACTBNA | BLCKGR | AbovePoverty | BelowPoverty | Total | PovertyRate |
|--------|---------|------|----------|--------|--------------|--------------|-------|-------------|
| 150 | 37 | 119 | 0007 | 1 | 531 | 161 | 692 | 23.3% |
| 150 | 37 | 119 | 0007 | 2 | 97 | 73 | 170 | 42.9% |
| 150 | 37 | 119 | 0008 | 1 | 1136 | 860 | 1996 | 43.1% |
| 150 | 37 | 119 | 0008 | 2 | 145 | 743 | 888 | 83.7% |
| 150 | 37 | 119 | 0009 | 1 | 1083 | 176 | 1259 | 14.0% |
| 150 | 37 | 119 | 0009 | 2 | 439 | 244 | 683 | 35.7% |
| 150 | 37 | 119 | 0009 | 3 | 229 | 152 | 381 | 39.9% |
| 150 | 37 | 119 | 0010 | 1 | 748 | 51 | 799 | 6.4% |
| 150 | 37 | 119 | 0010 | 2 | 615 | 99 | 714 | 13.9% |
| 150 | 37 | 119 | 0010 | 3 | 730 | 198 | 928 | 21.3% |
| 150 | 37 | 119 | 0011 | 1 | 860 | 152 | 1012 | 15.0% |
| 150 | 37 | 119 | 0011 | 2 | 841 | 128 | 969 | 13.2% |
| 150 | 37 | 119 | 0011 | 3 | 525 | 46 | 571 | 8.1% |
| 150 | 37 | 119 | 0011 | 4 | 150 | 52 | 202 | 25.7% |
| 150 | 37 | 119 | 0012 | 1 | 2024 | 271 | 2295 | 11.8% |
| 150 | 37 | 119 | 0012 | 2 | 1077 | 65 | 1142 | 5.7% |
| 150 | 37 | 119 | 0012 | 3 | 884 | 40 | 924 | 4.3% |
| 150 | 37 | 119 | 0012 | 4 | 361 | 62 | 423 | 14.7% |
| 150 | 37 | 119 | 0013 | 1 | 205 | 15 | 220 | 6.8% |
| 150 | 37 | 119 | 0013 | 2 | 169 | 5 | 174 | 2.9% |
| 150 | 37 | 119 | 0013 | 3 | 1720 | 260 | 1980 | 13.1% |
| 150 | 37 | 119 | 0013 | 4 | 907 | 123 | 1030 | 11.9% |

Record: 1 of 399

Microsoft Access - [MecklenburgPoverty : Select Query]
File Edit View Insert Format Records Tools Window Help
Datasheet View · NUM

Using data from the 2000 Census, the *Observer's* reporter calculated poverty rates for the block groups in Mecklenburg County. The Poverty Rate field, at the right side of this table, shows the calculated percentage for each block group.

## More questions

There was more: the reporter found that switching to a neighborhood school system would reduce the distance nonmagnet school children travel to school, especially African American children. Around 42 percent of African American children were bused past their nearest schools, compared to 23 percent for white children. Further, the reporter used the GIS to find that moving to a neighborhood school system would cut the median travel distance for African Americans to .6 mile from 1.9 miles, and for whites to .5 mile from 1 mile.

Next the reporter wanted to answer some questions about schools: What would a neighborhood school system do to racial diversity? How impoverished would each school's student body be? And what effect would the change have on school crowding?

To answer the first question, the reporter began by calculating a racial-diversity score, a number that measures the probability that two students picked at random from a school would be of a different race, for each school.

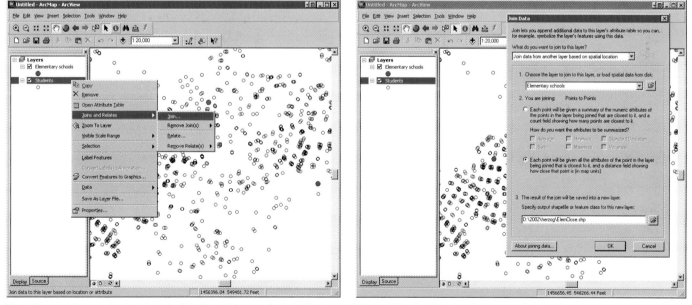

The *Observer's* reporter had to calculate the distances that students would travel to school under a nearest-school assignment system and then under the system of busing in place at the time. The reporter used Atlas GIS software to do this; the illustrations on this page show how to achieve the same results in ArcView 8.x. The first step is to show the nearest school assignments. That starts with what's called a "spatial join" (left) between the school points and the student points layers. The spatial join determines which school is the closest for each student and calculates the distance to that school (right).

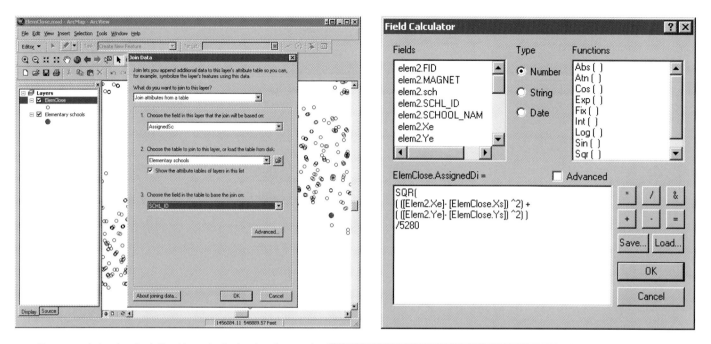

The second step is calculating the actual school assignments. In ArcView 8.x that begins with joining the data in the school point layer to the student points layer table (top). Then, a new field is created to store the distance from school using a formula (top, far right). The resulting table (right) lists for each student the closest school in the first column and the distance to that school in the second column. The third column lists for each student the actual school assigned and the fourth column contains that distance. These basic steps create the data needed to compare average travel times to school in the Charlotte–Mecklenburg district.

## Stark conclusions

After running census figures through the racial-diversity index, the reporter found that the Charlotte–Mecklenburg schools were twice as integrated as the neighborhoods in the county. About half of the county's schools would have little or no racial diversity if desegregation ended and students were assigned to their closest schools. And the number of schools ranking low on diversity or having none would jump to 64 from 19.

By analyzing the student poverty weights, the *Observer* found that neighborhood assignments would create a group of super-poor schools in the inner cities. By comparing the student assignments to school capacity figures, the reporter found that about thirty-nine thousand students would attend overcrowded schools, with the problem being particularly severe in the inner-city neighborhoods.

To help readers understand the impact of the findings, the *Observer* published side-by-side maps comparing schools by the different variables in 1998 and under the neighborhood schools plan. Readers could easily see, for instance, how poverty would differ by school.

A federal judge that September ruled that the school system no longer was unconstitutionally segregated as it had been decades before. He ordered an end to the school system's policy of using race to make school assignments. The ruling forced the district to abandon the busing of children to achieve integration. Many of the findings published by the *Observer* in the January 1999 series became central issues in the public debate surrounding the design of a new school system. Community leaders, during public meetings, cited the paper's findings.

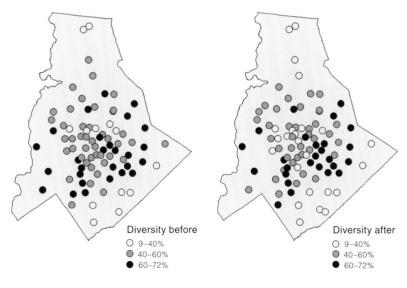

**Diversity before**
○ 9–40%
◉ 40–60%
● 60–72%

**Diversity after**
○ 9–40%
◉ 40–60%
● 60–72%

These ArcView maps compare school diversity under busing (left) and under a system of neighborhood student assignments (right). Schools shown as yellow dots have diversity scores of 9 to 40 percent; schools shown with green dots have diversity scores of 40 to 60 percent, and schools shown with blue dots have diversity scores of 60 to 72 percent. The maps show that the number of low-diversity schools (yellow dots) would increase if the district assigned students to neighborhood schools.

The *Observer* bolstered some of its "Deciding Desegregation" coverage by publishing maps that illustrated the characteristics of the schools under busing and how they would be under a new student assignment system. The top set of maps compares crowding as it was (left) with how it would be (right) if the district shifted students to their closest schools. Gray dots show the schools at less than 80 percent capacity; white dots show those at 80 to 120 percent, and the black dots show those at 120 percent and above. The maps showed that inner-city schools would become more crowded if the district assigned children to neighborhood schools. The set of maps at bottom shows that many inner-city schools would have greater rates of poor students if children attended neighborhood schools. The map at bottom left shows schools with busing in place; the map at bottom right shows a greater number of black circles indicating poverty levels increasing.

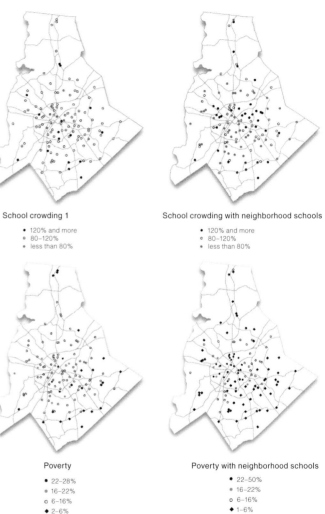

School crowding 1

- 120% and more
- 80–120%
- less than 80%

School crowding with neighborhood schools

- 120% and more
- 80–120%
- less than 80%

Poverty

- 22–28%
- 16–22%
- 6–16%
- 2–6%

Poverty with neighborhood schools

- 22–50%
- 16–22%
- 6–16%
- 1–6%

## GIS in service

The *Observer* used GIS again when the school administration proposed a new system of neighborhood schools that aimed to assign children to the closest schools. As a public service the newspaper in November 1999 published a twelve-page special section that showed all fourteen proposed high school attendance areas and, inside each, the attendance areas for the middle and elementary schools. The *Observer's* reporter helped generate the maps using ArcView GIS. He overlaid a streets shapefile, a point file showing the location of schools, and an area file showing the attendance zones. Parents attending the public hearings about the proposed school zones took copies of the section along as a reference. When the district revised the attendance areas the following month, the *Observer* published another special section with maps created in ArcView.

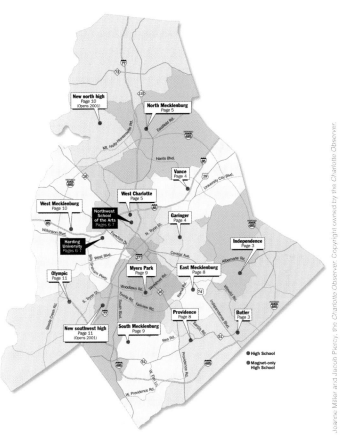

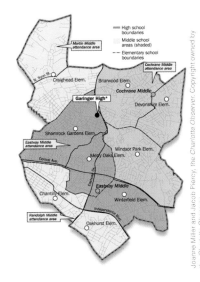

A map showing the Charlotte–Mecklenburg School District (top) ran on the cover of the *Observer's* November 1999 special section explaining the district's proposed student assignment plan. Inside the section, the paper published maps (example at left) showing the boundaries of each assignment zone and the schools within them.

## Award-winning coverage

The *Observer's* reporting, bolstered by GIS, played a key role in informing parents as the school system went through enormous, historic change. The series published in January 1999 was part of the "Deciding Desegregation" continuing coverage that won first prize for breaking or hard news in the 1999 national Education Writers Association contest.

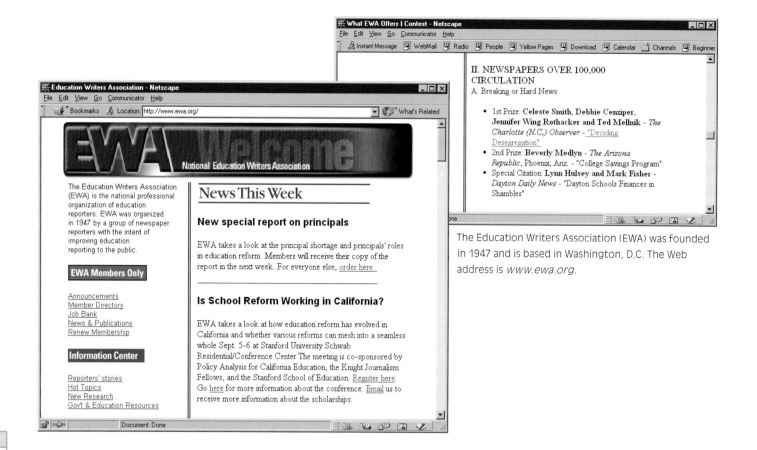

The Education Writers Association (EWA) was founded in 1947 and is based in Washington, D.C. The Web address is *www.ewa.org*.

## Acknowledgments

Ted Mellnik
Database Editor, the *Charlotte Observer*
For providing information about the use of GIS in reporting about school assignments, and for providing program screen shots, map graphics, and newspaper copies.

Sheilita K. Douglas
Executive Assistant to the Editor, the *Charlotte Observer*
For providing permission to reprint maps and photos.

Lisa King
Executive Director of the Education Writers Association
For Web graphics reprint permission.

# 4 *Plotting pockets of lead poisoning*

Across the United States some one million children have high levels of lead in their bloodstreams. Lead poisoning is particularly acute in the old cities of the Northeast, where children living in deteriorating old homes swallow lead paint chips or inhale particles so tiny that they float in the air, invisible to the naked eye. In 1998, a leading environmental lawyer in New England labeled Providence, Rhode Island, the "lead poison capital" of the United States. Nearly three thousand children are poisoned every year in Rhode Island, the smallest of the fifty states.

Lead poisoning can damage a child's kidneys and cause high blood pressure. The lead also can lower a child's IQ and contribute to a host of other ills: hearing and speech problems, hyperactivity, and learning disabilities. Most poisoned children in Rhode Island get tested regularly in public health clinics or their pediatricians' offices. Some of those children need to be hospitalized and receive intravenous doses of medicine that flush out the lead stored in their bones. After the alarm over the child lead poisoning epidemic got louder in 1998, the *Providence Journal,* the largest newspaper in Rhode Island, decided to take its own look at lead poisoning rates across the state.

### Scrutiny begins

While poisoning rates overall had been declining for years, thanks largely to the federal government's ban on adding lead to gasoline and paint, neighborhood activists protested that poisoning remained a scourge in the inner cities. Public health authorities and political leaders began to press harder for programs to prevent lead poisoning and rehabilitate the old, dilapidated housing that still harbored remnants of lead paint.

For a news story, the reporter needed to answer two simple, but critical questions: Where exactly did lead poisoning strike the hardest? Who lived in those neighborhoods? After getting answers the reporter could hit the streets and find out how public health authorities were reaching into these neighborhoods and trying to prevent the poisonings. GIS and public data—obtained at no cost to the newspaper—played a key role in answering those questions and getting the story started.

Under Rhode Island law, every child under the age of six is supposed to get tested for lead poisoning. Private doctors and public-health clinic workers draw blood from the children, have the samples tested, and report the results to the state Department of Health. The department enters the results into a database so workers can track the rise and fall of lead levels in the children's bloodstreams. In a typical year, workers for the department log the results for more than thirty-four thousand blood tests.

The *Journal's* reporter requested blood-test data under Rhode Island's open records law (which covers computerized records) but immediately hit a snag: the Department of Health declined to release the data because it contained the names and addresses of children. Disclosure would violate medical confidentiality guidelines.

After brief negotiations, the newspaper and the Department of Health arrived at a compromise that protected the identities of the children while allowing for release of the data: the department replaced the names of the children with a unique identifier—a combination of letters and numbers—that allowed the *Journal* reporter to see which children had more than one blood lead test. Also, the department replaced the child's home address at the time of the poisoning with a more general level of geography: the census tract.

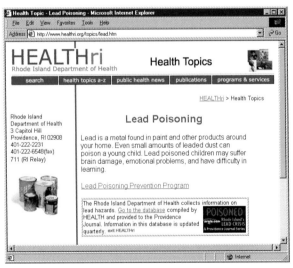

Some children get lead poisoning by eating old paint containing lead; others are poisoned by ingesting tiny particles of lead paint dust. The Rhode Island Department of Health is the key agency in the state's battle against child lead poisoning. Each year, the state collects data about more than thirty thousand child lead poisoning tests. The department's lead poisoning Web page is at *www.healthri.org/topics/lead.htm.*

## Identifying neighborhoods

Census tracts are geographic areas defined by the U.S. Census Bureau that typically contain about four thousand to eight thousand people. Tracts tend to follow real-world geographic features, such as major streets and rivers. In cities, the tracts often approximate neighborhoods.

With the data in hand, the reporter was ready to use his GIS program to create a map that would show which neighborhoods—as represented by census tracts—had the highest levels of lead poisoning. Because the database had this geographic element, it could be mapped.

First, the reporter had to get the data in shape. Using a database manager, he created a table listing a record for each tract and the percentage of children tested who were poisoned in 1997. He exported the table from the database manager, imported it into his GIS program, and then joined the data to the census tract layer, using the unique identification number for the tract.

Next, the *Journal* reporter used data from the 1990 Census to calculate the number of children under six years old in each tract. From that figure, the reporter calculated the percentage of all children under six who were poisoned.

A reporter ran a simple database query in Microsoft Access to generate a table that calculated the child lead-poisoning rate for each census tract. The reporter then imported the census tract result table from Microsoft Access into his GIS and added it to his project. He then joined the tract field in the results table (on the left) to the tract field in the mapping file table (on the right). That attached the results to the map.

The Rhode Island Department of Health released this data table (top left) of child lead test results to the *Providence Journal*. The department generated a unique ID number for each child to mask the identity of the children. The department also included in each data record the child's census tract. In Providence and many other cities, census tract boundaries (upper right) often approximate neighborhood boundaries.

## Integrating data, maps

In the GIS program, the reporter created one thematic map showing total percent of children poisoned by tract and another showing percent of the tested children who were poisoned. Just by looking at the map anyone could see the tracts with the worst rates were in the core of Rhode Island's biggest cities. In some neighborhoods, the lead poisoning rate ran as high as 30 percent of all the children tested. That answered the first question, about where the lead poisonings occurred. GIS also provided the answer to the second question, about who lived there.

The reporter next joined a table of demographic data from the 1990 Census to the tracts and, using the selection tool, picked the tracts with the highest poisoning rates. Then, looking at the selected records attached to the tracts, he saw that those neighborhoods had high concentrations of immigrants and minorities. Those findings became the springboard for an in-depth front-page Sunday story that showed the ravages of child lead poisoning in Rhode Island's inner cities and detailed how public agencies and social service groups responded to the challenge of reaching people from other countries, many of whom could not speak English.

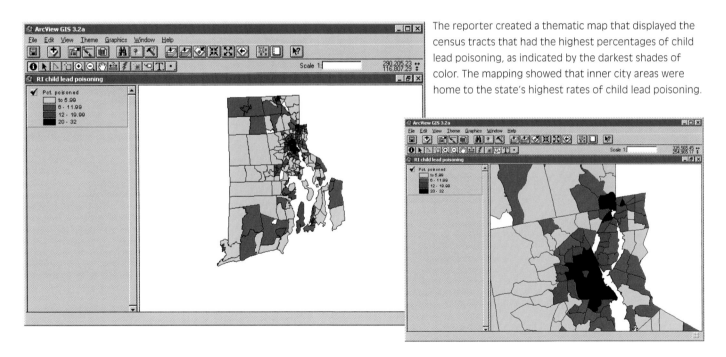

The reporter created a thematic map that displayed the census tracts that had the highest percentages of child lead poisoning, as indicated by the darkest shades of color. The mapping showed that inner city areas were home to the state's highest rates of child lead poisoning.

## Extending the analysis

When the *Providence Journal* revisited its child lead poisoning work three years later, the team of journalists working on the new project wanted to go beyond the analysis of 1997 neighborhood poisoning rates. This time, they wanted to plot the locations of homes where Department of Health environmental inspectors had discovered residential lead hazards.

The Department of Health gave the *Journal* a database of nearly thirteen hundred lead inspections from 1993 to 2000 that contained a wealth of information: property owner name, inspection result, abatement status of property, and—most important for the geographic analysis—the street address of the property.

Because the paper had the street addresses of the inspected locations, the reporter doing the GIS analysis could turn those addresses into a map layer that displayed the locations as individual points, and overlay that on a map of Rhode Island streets. The streets file already had been downloaded at no cost from the state GIS consortium's Web site. The reporter created the point map by geocoding the data using ArcView 3.2. During the geocoding process, ArcView evaluates every street address in a data file and attempts to find a match for it in the street address file. ArcView then adds the new point file as a map layer in a view.

That process displayed the location of the lead hazards across the state. But the reporter wanted to take the analysis a step further and see whether the paper could identify any "hot spots" or clusters of lead hazards.

A data table (left) from the state Department of Health tracked inspections of the homes of all children who had lead poisoning. The table had a street address field that could be mapped. After the reporter imported the lead inspection table into ArcView, he matched the inspections addresses to addresses in a streets map (center) using the geocoding function. That enabled him to create a point map (right) of the inspections.

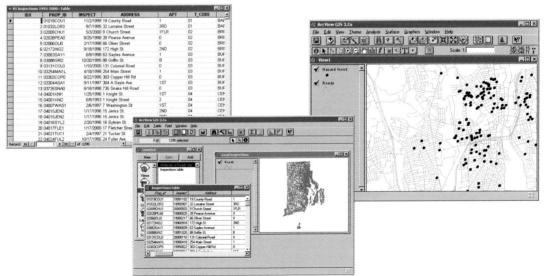

### Zeroing in

The reporter created the hot spots with ArcView Spatial Analyst, an ArcView extension that can be used to better understand spatial relationships in data. As it turned out, one of the largest hot spots identified by Spatial Analyst covered the south Providence neighborhood where one of the children who later would be featured in the newspaper's series had been poisoned.

The reporter also geocoded a table obtained at no cost from the statewide housing agency showing properties where low-interest loan proceeds were being used to abate lead hazards. The file, containing data about 350 loans, included the home address, owner, loan status, and loan amount. Overlaying the points on the inspections theme showed that many of the homes where inspectors had found lead hazards were getting cleaned up under the public program. It also showed that many homeowners were getting loans on their own, even before any children got poisoned.

ArcView Spatial Analyst helped to identify neighborhoods that had "hot spots" of child lead poisoning (above). A family featured in the *Providence Journal's* series had lived inside the "hot spot." The locations of lead hazards in the family's neighborhood were displayed in a graphic that ran with the series. The graphic was later reproduced (right) on the paper's Web site.

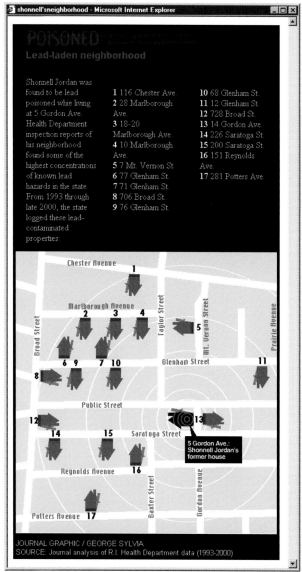

shonnell'sneighborhood - Microsoft Internet Explorer

POISONED
**Lead-laden neighborhood**

Shonnell Jordan was found to be lead poisoned whie living at 5 Gordon Ave. Health Department inspection reports of his neighborhood found some of the highest concentrations of known lead hazards in the state. From 1993 through late 2000, the state logged these lead-contaminated properties:

1 116 Chester Ave.
2 28 Marlborough Ave.
3 18-20 Marlborough Ave.
4 10 Marlborough Ave.
5 7 Mt. Vernon St.
6 77 Glenham St.
7 71 Glenham St.
8 706 Broad St.
9 76 Glenham St.
10 68 Glenham St.
11 12 Glenham St.
12 728 Broad St.
13 14 Gordon Ave.
14 226 Saratoga St.
15 200 Saratoga St.
16 151 Reynolds Ave.
17 281 Potters Ave.

5 Gordon Ave.: Shonnell Jordan's former house

JOURNAL GRAPHIC / GEORGE SYLVIA
SOURCE: Journal analysis of R.I. Health Department data (1993-2000)

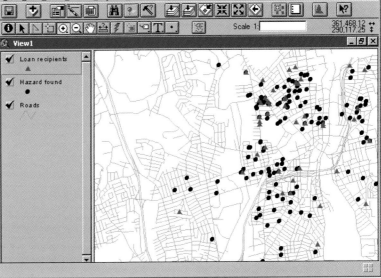

**Microsoft Excel - lead loan database [Read-Only]**

File Edit View Insert Format Tools Data Window Help

Arial  ▼ 9 ▼  **B** *I* U

F2  = JAMES P

| | D | E | F | G | H | I | J |
|---|---|---|---|---|---|---|---|
| 1 | AMT | LNAME | FNAME | Number | Street1 | Street2 | City |
| 2 | $ 42,970 | MARTEL SR | JAMES P | 87-89 | LEDGE STREET | 91 LEDGE STREET | CENTRAL FALLS |
| 3 | $ 32,950 | PECKHAM | WALLACE W | 36 | GARFIELD STREET | | CENTRAL FALLS |
| 4 | $ 18,953 | RAMIREZ | RENE | 53 | EARLE STREET | | CENTRAL FALLS |
| 5 | $ 47,250 | ALVES | LUIS A | 71 - 73 | HENRY STREET | | CENTRAL FALLS |
| 6 | $ 15,000 | HALL | JOSEPH | 200 | RUGGLES AVENUE | | NEWPORT |
| 7 | $ 15,000 | O'SULLIVAN | THOMAS | 22 | NARRAGANSETT STRE | | NEWPORT |
| 8 | $ 13,561 | CINOTTI | MARK A | 21 | CARROLL AVENUE | | NEWPORT |
| 9 | $ 27,650 | KEAVENEY | GERARD C | 11 | GIBBS AVENUE | | NEWPORT |
| 10 | $ 12,927 | WINDLEY | DAVID A | 25 | CAREY STREET | | NEWPORT |
| 11 | $ 2,195 | WALSH | PATRICK | 34 | BERKELEY AVENUE | | NEWPORT |
| 12 | $ 4,675 | WILKS III | ROBERT J | 19 | GRACE STREET | | CRANSTON |
| 13 | $ 13,200 | SALO | WAYNE A | 14 | WHIPPLE AVENUE | | CRANSTON |
| 14 | $ 47,250 | MELENDEZ | MARIA | 51-53 | DETROIT AVENUE | | PROVIDENCE |
| 15 | $ 4,725 | PACHECO | JOHN B | 46 | OLIVER STREET | | NORTH PROVIDI |
| 16 | $ 17,645 | COUTU | MICHAEL B | 120-122 | ARMISTICE BLVD | | PAWTUCKET |
| 17 | $ 46,746 | GORDON | SCOTT | 45-49 | SUMNER STREET | | PAWTUCKET |
| 18 | $ 2,870 | ZUROMSKI | PETER F. | 113-117 | SUFFOLK AVENUE | | PAWTUCKET |
| 19 | $ 25,514 | HUNTER | SAMUEL W. | 61-63 | DANIELS STREET | | PAWTUCKET |
| 20 | $ 72,361 | BURT | RAYMOND D. | 457 | MINERAL SPRING AVEN | | PAWTUCKET |
| 21 | $ 14,750 | THOMPSON-RE | MARY PATRICI | 167 | MAIN STREET | | |
| 22 | $ 15,000 | FREEMER III | ROBERT P | 54B | WESTMINSTER STREE | | |

Lead / LEADINFO /

Ready

This data table in Microsoft Excel (above) shows lead hazard abatement loans to homeowners. It includes street address information that can be mapped using geocoding, a function in GIS programs. The *Providence Journal's* reporter geocoded the abatement loan addresses and overlaid the results on top of the streets and lead hazards layers (right).

**ArcView GIS 3.2a**

File Edit View Theme Analysis Surface Graphics Window Help

Scale 1:

361,468.12
290,117.25

**View1**

✓ Loan recipients ▲

✓ Hazard found ●

✓ Roads

## Award-winning series

All of these discoveries—made possible by the GIS analysis—helped to bolster a six-day series in May 2001 that looked at the challenges facing lead-poisoned children and their families and detailed the lead poisoning death of a two-year-old Sudanese immigrant girl in New Hampshire.

The week the series ran, the state Department of Health announced tougher new rules that would allow the department to inspect more homes with suspected lead hazards. In the months after the series ran, the manager of the property where the Sudanese toddler died pleaded guilty to federal charges that he had failed to warn tenants of lead paint hazards and later tried to hide that omission from investigators. That same day the U.S. Environmental Protection Agency announced that it would start conducting inspections throughout New England to determine whether landlords were complying with the federal disclosure laws.

GIS helped to lay the foundation for a six-part series in the *Providence Journal* that examined the child lead poisoning problem in Rhode Island. The *Journal* posted the series on the Web at *www.projo.com/extra/lead* (right). As a public service, the newspaper posted the inspection database on the Web (left) and allowed users to look up the results.

The *Journal's* series won several awards, including honors in two New England regional contests, and placed as a runner-up for the Casey Medal for Meritorious Journalism, a national award presented by the Casey Journalism Center on Children and Families, at the University of Maryland's Philip Merrill College of Journalism.

*Runner-up:*
Peter B. Lord and John Freidah, *The Providence Journal,* for "Poisoned."
*Judges' comments:* A poignant, informative and surprising tale of how lead poisoning has affected many Rhode Island families.

The Casey Journalism Center on Children and Families is on the Web at *www.casey.umd.edu/home.nsf.*

**Acknowledgments**

Colleen Caron
Chief of Health Communications, Rhode Island Department of Health
For granting permission to reproduce graphic of state Health Department child lead poisoning Web page.

Corinna Ulrich
Assistant General Counsel, Belo Corp.
For granting permission to reproduce Web screen shots from projo.com.

Betty Pearce
Administrative Director, Casey Journalism Center on Children and Families
For granting permission to reproduce graphic of Casey Center Web site.

# 5 *Mapping bars and fatal crashes*

Across the United States, more than seventeen thousand people die every year in drunken-driving accidents and 310,000 are injured, according to the National Highway Transportation Safety Administration. That's about two deaths and thirty-five injuries an hour. And, despite decades of awareness campaigns and political pressure from public health and interest groups, drunken-driving fatalities increased nearly 5 percent in 2000—the largest single-year increase in more than a decade—and inched up even further in 2001. Groups such as Mothers Against Drunk Driving have been pushing lawmakers in every state to adopt a .08 percent blood-alcohol concentration as the legal benchmark for intoxication. A federal law signed in 2000 set that as the new national standard and threatens to cut off federal road-building funds from any states that fail to comply by 2004.

Journalists have written about drunken driving before, identifying repeat offenders or exposing flaws in the courts. Reporters for the *Philadelphia Inquirer* newspaper—moved by anecdotal accounts of tragic accidents in their region—had wanted to do an in-depth report about drunken driving. They knew that other journalists had already reported extensively and wanted to bring a fresh approach to examining the problem. That cutting-edge approach turned out to rely heavily on GIS.

### Searching online

When they started laying the groundwork for their project, the *Philadelphia Inquirer* reporters wanted to find out how the leading researchers were examining drunken driving. So they plunged into online database and Web research. They searched medical and other academic journal indexes to locate the latest studies about drunken driving and trekked to a university library to track down hard-to-locate journal articles. During their background research, something caught their attention: studies that used GIS and spatial statistics to look for connections between drinking establishments and drunken driving accidents.

One of the journalists, a computer-assisted reporting specialist, decided to map the liquor license locations and drunken driving accidents in the five main Pennsylvania counties that the *Inquirer* covers. But first, she needed the data for the reporting.

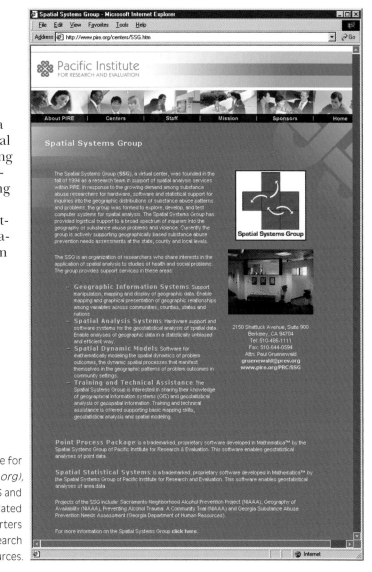

Researchers at the Pacific Institute for Research and Evaluation *(www.pire.org)*, based in Berkeley, California, use GIS and spatial statistics to study alcohol-related and drunken-driving questions. Reporters at the *Inquirer* relied on the research group as one of their sources.

The reporters already had been trying to obtain detailed accident data from the Pennsylvania Department of Transportation (PennDOT), but had little luck. In previous years, PennDOT had released data about accidents, but always excluded details about the exact locations of the crashes. Then, in 1999, PennDOT stripped out even more information from public versions of the databases. Members of the public—journalists included—no longer got details about the age of the driver, injuries, and whether alcohol was involved. The computer-assisted reporting specialist and an editor traveled to Harrisburg, the state capital, and appealed to the secretary of the Department of Transportation, but the department did not budge. Instead, the department provided state road alcohol-related accident and fatality totals for the cities, boroughs, and townships in the *Inquirer's* coverage area.

The Pennsylvania Department of Transportation (PennDOT) collects data about alcohol-related crashes and fatalities.

The *Inquirer* focused its reporting inside the five-county portion of the Philadelphia metropolitan area that's in southeastern Pennsylvania.

### Acquiring data

Around the same time the *Inquirer's* journalists were doing their background research, they started to draw on sources in the newspaper's reporting area.

Sources inside PennDOT quietly provided a copy of a Microsoft Excel spreadsheet that contained alcohol-related crash data for all state-maintained roads in the five-county Philadelphia metropolitan area. The data, for 1995 through 1999, had accident and DUI accident details for five-mile road segments. It included the state route number, total number of DUI accidents, number of people killed in DUI accidents, and length of road segment. The spreadsheet also contained a road segment identifier that could be used in a GIS program to map the DUI accident data by road segment.

After getting this data from their sources, the journalists formally asked PennDOT officials for the data for 1996 through 2000. They decided to focus on the 619 road segments that had at least five alcohol-related crashes. The computer-assisted reporting specialist downloaded shapefiles of the PennDOT road segments from the Internet. She wanted to join the accidents data to the streets file. She was unable to join the tables immediately because the streets segment identifier was stored differently in the streets file and the accident data file. ArcView joins require fields whose contents can be matched exactly.

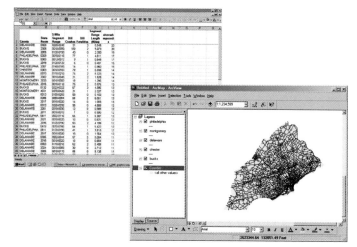

Reporters at the *Inquirer* obtained a Microsoft Excel spreadsheet (above left) with information about all alcohol-related crashes and fatalities for the state-maintained roads in their coverage area for 1996 to 2000. Each row of the spreadsheet listed a segment and included the number of drunken driving accidents and fatalities. The *Inquirer's* reporters worked with a shapefile (above right) of all state-maintained roads in ArcView 8.x.

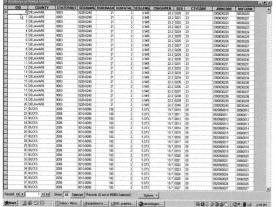

After getting the latest version of the alcohol-related crash data table, the *Inquirer's* reporters imported it into ArcView.

Specifically, the problem was this: The ID in the data table was reported as a range. In the map table, each segment had its own ID number. So a colleague wrote a Perl script that converted the ranges in the data table to individual identification numbers. Perl is a freely available programming language used to process text, among other things. After joining the tables, the reporters created a thematic map showing the number of DUI fatalities per mile for the road segments.

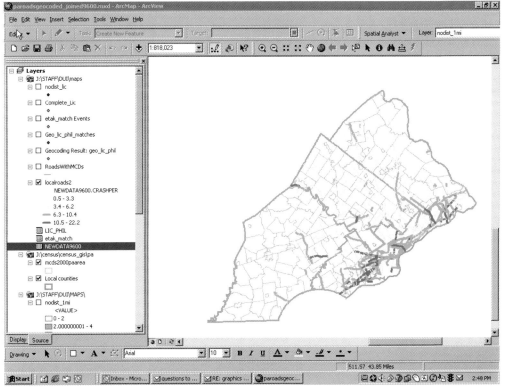

By color-coding the street segments by the rate of alcohol-related crashes, the *Inquirer* was able to see which segments were the most dangerous. The roads colored orange had 10.5 to 22.2 alcohol-related crashes per mile, and the ones colored gold had 6.3 to 10.4 such crashes.

## Overlaying data

The *Inquirer's* journalists could have stopped there and written a story about the stretches of state roads with the highest concentrations of DUI fatalities. But they wanted to overlay data showing the highest concentrations of drinking establishments and look for potential patterns.

When the newspaper's computer-assisted reporting specialist turned to this part of the GIS analysis, it became clear that ArcView 8.x alone could not provide the answers. The liquor license data with records of four thousand license locations in the Philadelphia metropolitan area would translate into a lot of little dots on the map. So after talking with some researchers and GIS experts and taking an ESRI software class, she decided to use Spatial Analyst, an ArcView extension. ArcView extensions expand the capabilities of the program. Among other things, Spatial Analyst analyzes points to create map layers that show densities. In this case, the computer-assisted reporting specialist wanted to show the liquor license densities per square mile.

The *Inquirer* needed to turn the addresses of four thousand licensed drinking establishments into a point map before it could use the advanced features of Spatial Analyst.

Before using Spatial Analyst, she needed to create a point map showing the location of the drinking establishments. The state's Liquor Control Board had provided the licensee data to the newspaper on CD–ROM at no cost. The computer-assisted reporting specialist imported the data into ArcView and she and a colleague used its geocoding function. Geocoding matches the street addresses stored in a data table to the street address and address range in a streets map file. It then places a point in the map along the appropriate spot in the street segment. ArcView geocoded most of the four thousand licensee records—80 percent of the total—using a street map file from the U.S. Census Bureau. Geocoding match rates often depend on the accuracy and comprehensiveness of the street files used. While U.S. Census Bureau street maps are good for geocoding, enhanced maps provided by commercial services often are more complete and accurate. So the *Inquirer* journalists geocoded the remaining records using Tele Atlas, a commercial service.

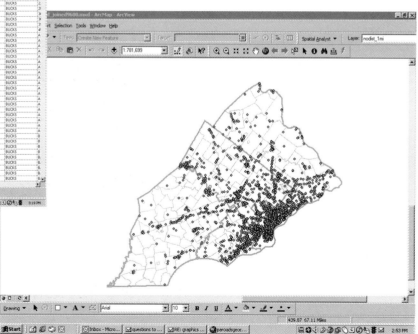

After ArcView geocoded the liquor license locations, it created a new table (above) with the results. The status field of the table tells whether ArcView matched (M) or failed to match (U) the address against a streets map table. After geocoding, the *Inquirer* had a point map (right) of all the licensed drinking establishments. However, with all the points on the map it was difficult to find the highest concentrations of establishments.

## Refining the analysis

After reading the Spatial Analyst documentation and consulting with experts some more, the computer-assisted reporting specialist settled on using the Kernel Density function to create a density map of the liquor license locations. The kernel procedure estimates densities based upon the patterns in a point layer. The resulting image shows the estimated densities. The experts guided her through the process of setting the search radius, area units, and output cell size parameters in Spatial Analyst.

When the reporters added the layer to the display, little blobs with shaded rings sprawled across the Philadelphia metropolitan area. Those blobs displayed the concentrations of liquor license locations. Then they added the streets file, with the streets shaded by rate of fatal DUI accidents. The map on the computer screen showed most of the accidents happened around concentrations of drinking establishments. The *Inquirer* had a story—one that no newspaper had ever discovered using computer tools.

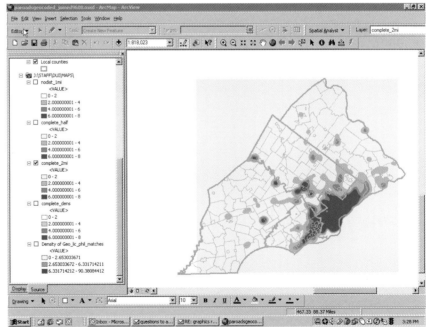

The *Inquirer* used ArcView Spatial Analyst, an ArcView extension, to create a density map to show the highest concentrations of licensed drinking establishments. The *Inquirer's* reporters entered parameters in Spatial Analyst's dialog boxes to calculate the density.

After Spatial Analyst calculated the density of drinking establishments, it drew a map layer that clearly showed the greatest concentrations.

## Checking information

As exciting as the discovery was, the *Inquirer* wanted to be sure that its analysis was solid. The computer-assisted reporting specialist made copies of the ArcView map document files and sent them to two researchers who perform spatial analyses of drunken driving. All of the feedback indicated that the newspaper's work was solid. But the *Inquirer* followed one suggestion: remove liquor license concentrations of less than two per square mile from the density layer.

That simplified the map. So did limiting the street segments that were displayed and symbolizing them by only two accident rate categories: high (10.5 to 22.2 accidents per square mile) shaded as orange, and above average (6.3 to 10.4 accidents per mile) shaded as gold. Once that was done, the *Inquirer's* computer-assisted reporting specialist gave a map document to the newspaper's graphic artist, who produced a map for the series, "Loaded for Trouble," which ran in June 2002.

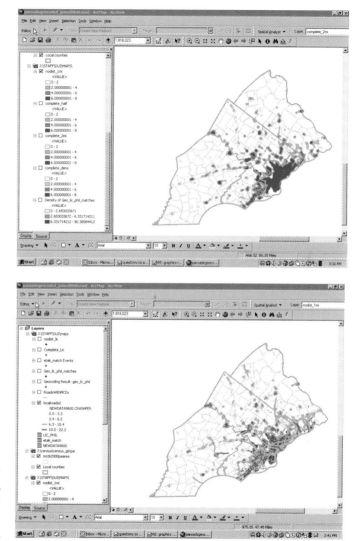

The *Inquirer's* reporters used the ArcView Legend Editor to eliminate liquor license densities of less than two per square mile (top map). When the paper's journalists displayed the drinking establishment density with the roads file, symbolized by accident rates, they could see clear patterns (bottom map).

A graphic artist at the *Inquirer* took the map document file and used it to create this graphic that ran in the newspaper. Red lines indicate roads with high accident rates, while green lines indicate roads with above average accident rates.

The *Philadelphia Inquirer's* June 23, 2002, edition provided major coverage of DUI "hot spots," and it pointed readers to an inside map "that could save your life." The map was developed in part with GIS.

## Interactive tools

The *Inquirer*'s map couldn't show the exact accident rate of every stretch—just the range—so the newspaper used ArcIMS® 3 software to give readers the opportunity to get more detailed information at the paper's Web site. The goal: give readers the power to zoom in on their neighborhoods and learn the accident rates.

ArcIMS is ESRI's tool to serve interactive maps on the Web, and it can utilize the same mapping shapefiles that journalists use in their news reporting. The Web editor at the *Inquirer* loaded the shapefiles and

configured ArcIMS. First, he converted the density layer created by Spatial Analyst from a raster (image) file into a shapefile. Then, he loaded that new shapefile along with the streets shapefile into ArcIMS. He also downloaded ESRI's Site Starter Application set of Active Server Page (ASP) applications from the ESRI Web site and customized one to add directional navigation. He also modified the code so a user could click any road segment with the identifier tool and see the name of the road and fatal accident rate inside a box.

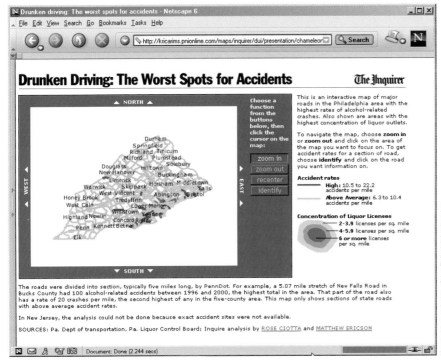

The *Inquirer* used ArcIMS to make its map interactive and provide readers with more localized information than a graphic could provide.

The Web map took a couple of days to configure and attracted even more attention from people who had read the newspaper's series. Visitors to the *Inquirer's* Web site could use a calculator to enter information and get an estimated blood-alcohol level, and view drunken driving accident and arrest statistics by town.

In the days that the series ran, readers reacted by posting messages to an online bulletin board on the Web site. A friend of a woman killed in a drunken driving accident urged Pennsylvania and New Jersey lawmakers to adopt the .08 percent blood-alcohol threshold, while others questioned the effectiveness of that approach. Others thanked the *Inquirer* for its groundbreaking stories and keeping drunken-driving fatalities in the public eye.

These maps show how readers could zoom in on specific areas and identify particular roads to find out the rates of alcohol-related accidents.

## Acknowledgments

Rose Ciotta
Editor for computer-assisted reporting, the *Philadelphia Inquirer*
For providing information and graphics for this case study.

Matt Ericson
Graphics Editor, the *New York Times*, formerly with the *Philadelphia Inquirer*
For providing information for this case study.

Anne Gordon
Managing Editor, the *Philadelphia Inquirer*
For granting permission to reproduce Web and newspaper graphics.

# 6 *Linking race and spoiled ballots*

The 2000 U.S. presidential election was the most contested race for the White House in history. Even after the polls closed on November 7, people across the United States watched their televisions in anticipation as the shifting Florida ballot count made it clear that the race between Republican George W. Bush and Democrat Al Gore in that state wouldn't be decided on election night. Without Florida, neither candidate had enough electoral votes to claim victory. So the winner in Florida would be the victor in the race for the presidency.

Political operatives for both candidates fanned across the state, mounting challenges in court and election offices in counties where voters—some confused by ill-designed ballots—failed to cast their votes properly. As the nation's media scrutinized the Florida elections and balloting procedures, it became clear to many that electoral problems abounded across the state. At the *Washington Post*, reporters and editors used GIS to help understand what happened.

### Disturbing claims

Not long after election day, the *Washington Post* started to examine claims that the ballots cast by African-American voters had been rejected at higher rates than whites because of voting errors. Many African Americans had gone to the polls for the first time, answering the call of the National Association for the Advancement of Colored People (NAACP) Voter Empowerment Program. Across the United States, the number of African-American voters increased by two million and the turnout set a national record. In Florida alone, 893,000 African Americans voted—40 percent of them for the first time, the *Post* reported. Though the NAACP does not endorse candidates, exit polls in Florida have shown African Americans voting in favor of Democratic Party candidates more than 90 percent of the time.

Did their votes count as much as those cast by white voters? The *Post* set out to answer that question.

One of the paper's reporters had used GIS to analyze election results and racial patterns in two Florida counties years earlier while reporting for the *Miami Herald*. He decided to look at the results by precincts—small voting areas—to look for patterns that might get obscured by a county-level study. He knew that the *Post* could easily obtain the data it needed and use GIS to explore any potential connections between race and ballot "spoilage"—the rate at which the punch card ballots had been disqualified—at the precinct level.

Florida's largest counties used the punch cards in the 2000 general election. Ballots with more than one hole punched for presidential candidates were considered "overvotes" and rejected by the vote-reading machines. Ballots with a hole improperly punched were considered "undervotes" and also were rejected.

For its initial reporting, the *Post* focused on Miami–Dade and Duval counties, two urban counties that rank among the top ten in Florida in terms of population. Nine percent of the ballots in Duval County, which is home to the city of Jacksonville, had no vote for president, the *Post* had reported two days after the election.

Election precincts, shown here in ArcView 3.2, are small, neighborhood-level voting areas. Journalists can examine results at the precinct level if they can obtain election data from local authorities.

The *Washington Post's* online news content is on the Web at *www.washingtonpost.com,* and additional information about the paper is available at *www.washpost.com.*

## Studying racial data

The *Post's* reporter jumped into the reporting with ArcView 3.2 by looking for the mapping shapefiles and data files on the Web. He found a statewide precinct map in ArcView shapefile format on the Florida Legislature's Web site and downloaded it. The shapefile included data about the race of registered voters in each precinct. Florida collects the race information because the election procedures in some of its counties come under the scrutiny of the U.S. Justice Department pursuant to the federal Voting Rights Act of 1965. Under that law, the Justice Department is supposed to review any proposed changes to voting procedures and ensure that they would not disenfranchise minority voters.

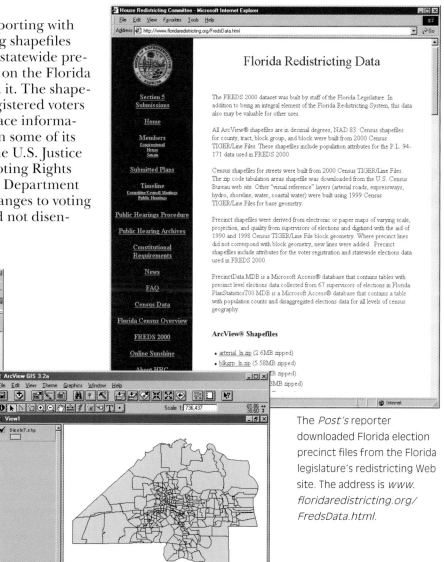

The *Post's* reporter used the precinct shapefile (map right) for Duval County to explore patterns between voter registration by race and high concentrations of invalidated paper ballots. The precinct shapefile included voter registration, election, racial, political party, and gender data. This is a view of the table in ArcView (above).

The *Post's* reporter downloaded Florida election precinct files from the Florida legislature's redistricting Web site. The address is *www.floridaredistricting.org/FredsData.html*.

### Combining data

Duval County provided its over- and undervote data files to the *Post* reporter. He used another program to stitch the files into a text file that he then imported into ArcView.

He wanted to create a map with two layers: one to display the rate of ballot spoilage by precinct, showing the values as graduated colors, and another to display polygons that ringed the areas with high percentages of registered African-American voters.

To map the first layer, which showed the spoilage rates, the reporter joined the election results table with the table for the precincts map, using the unique precinct identification field. Then he used the precinct theme Legend Editor to symbolize the spoilage rate by precinct using a red-to-dark red scheme.

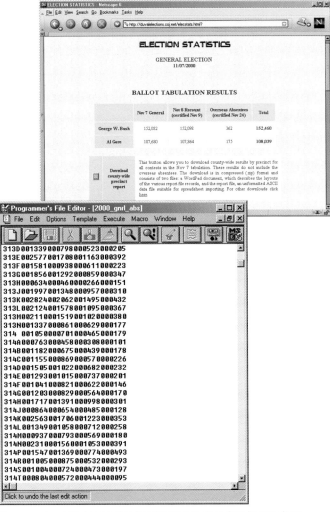

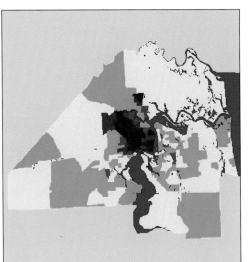

Using ArcView, the reporter created a Duval County map (right) that displayed the rates of invalidated ballots by precinct as shaded red. The deeper the shade of red, the higher the percentage of invalidated ballots.

The reporter obtained ballot invalidation status data by precinct from Duval County. The data is now available on the Web at *duvalelections.coj.net/elecstats.html*. The data came as a text file, shown here in a text-editing program.

To create polygons that outlined the two types of majority African-American precincts, the *Post's* reporter went through several steps. First, he opened the table for the precincts layer and used the query tool to select all of the precincts with more than 50 percent African-American registered voters (main image, top). Then he entered a formula into the field calculator that placed "50" in the Blackgrp field he had created to hold the values for the two African-American majority levels (box at lower left). Then he repeated those two steps, substituting "70" in the field calculator formula to signify areas with greater than 70 percent African-American voter registration. Last, he used the ArcView summary function to merge the precincts into a polygon shapefile containing three polygons: one for each voter level and another for the areas where African Americans were in the minority in voter registration (box at lower right).

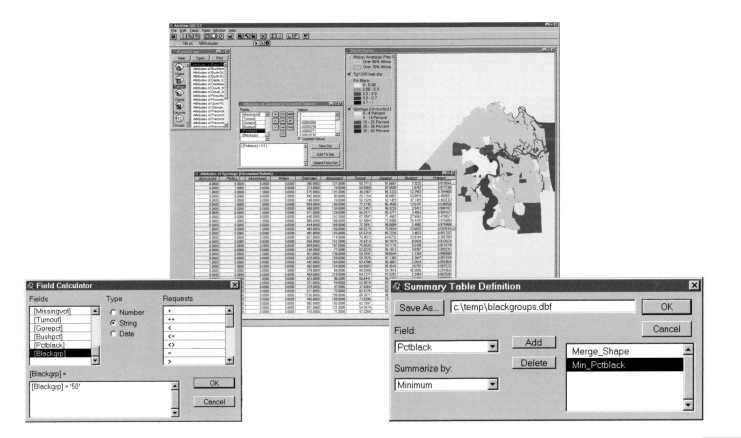

## Mapping results

After adding the new theme to the display, he used the Legend Editor to create transparent polygons with colored outlines to show the areas with high levels of African-American registered voters. The high African-American majority areas were colored bright green and the majority areas light green. The African-American precincts lined up perfectly with the precincts having high spoilage rates. The *Post* got the same results after mapping the elections data for Miami–Dade County. The analysis showed that the vote rejection rates were not random.

In early December, the *Post* reporter and a colleague wrote an article that told readers how the African-American and heavily Democratic neighborhoods in the two Florida counties had more votes rejected than in other areas in those counties. Black-and-white maps of Duval and Miami–Dade counties ran in the newspaper alongside the story. Why did those areas have higher spoilage rates? Elections experts interviewed by the *Post* said the new voters were more likely to be confused by the poorly designed ballots. So precincts with large numbers of new voters would have high spoilage rates. In addition, the paper found that African-American voters were somewhat more likely to live in areas where poll workers didn't check ballots immediately for errors and give voters the chance to correct them.

The *Post's* findings attracted national attention. On December 14—the day after Vice President Gore conceded the election to Bush—the *Post* reporter who did the GIS analysis appeared on CNN's Burden of Proof and talked about the ballot rejection rates by precinct.

When the reporter overlaid the theme outlining the areas with high percentages of African-American voters, it was easy to see how those areas also had the high ballot invalidation rates. The dark green lines show precincts where African Americans made up greater than 70 percent of registered voters, and the light green lines indicate areas where African Americans make up more than half to 70 percent of registered voters. The darkest red areas had at least 35 percent of their ballots containing no vote for president.

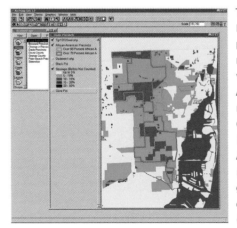

The GIS analysis for Miami–Dade County produced similar results. The precincts with majority African-American registrations (light green) and high majority African-American registrations (dark green) had high levels of ballot invalidation (the darker reds).

### Looking elsewhere

The *Post's* reporters also wanted to check whether other areas in the country had high levels of ballot spoilage in minority precincts. So they picked two big metropolitan areas where the same punch cards had been used in the 2000 presidential election: Chicago and suburban Cook County, and Atlanta, Georgia.

Chicago and Cook County both provided the election and ballot spoilage data at the precinct level. Election officials in Chicago provided a Microsoft Access database file and the reporter downloaded it. Cook County election authorities e-mailed the results to the reporter in a compressed text file. Both the city and county said they lacked GIS map files, so the *Post's* reporter downloaded 1995 voting district maps—which typically line up with precincts—from the U.S. Census Bureau in the bureau's proprietary TIGER file format. He converted the files into shapefiles using TGR2SHP, a utility sold by GIS Tools of Knoxville, Tennessee. The precinct identification number in the election data from the city and county matched the identification number in the voting district map from the Census, so the reporter easily joined them together. Then he used the Legend Editor to create a map that displayed the precinct spoilage rate by graduated reds; the deeper the red, the higher the rate of spoilage.

Chicago and Cook County lacked voter race data by precinct; neither fell under the Voting Rights Act enforcement, so elections authorities never collected it. The reporter decided to use data from the 1990 Census, the most recent demographic data available at the time, to calculate the percentage of African Americans. He also had to include Hispanics because he later uncovered high spoilage rates in largely Hispanic precincts.

Assigning racial information from the census block group layer to the precinct layer required some additional work. The reporter wanted to assign the data using a spatial join but could not do that because spatial joins can have only one polygon layer. So he had to turn one of the polygon themes into a point theme. He opened his precinct theme as a table and added two fields to hold each polygon's latitude and longitude. Employing the field calculator's Get X and Get Y commands, he calculated latitude and longitude coordinates. Once that was completed, he mapped the precincts as points in the display, along with the census block groups.

Then he performed a spatial join to assign demographic data from the block groups file to each voter precinct point. Using the Summarize function as he did with the Florida data, the reporter created a polygon shapefile outlining the precincts having a minority population of at least 95 percent. (The reporter used a high percentage in Chicago and Cook county after finding that the level of segregation left minority proportions either extremely high or extremely low.)

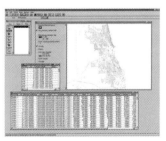

To attach census demographic block group data to the precincts, the *Post's* reporter first converted all of the Chicago and Cook County precinct polygons to points (symbolized as green for Chicago in this view). Next, he performed a spatial join to assign the block group data to the precincts.

### Similar analysis

The reporter, using the Legend Editor, displayed the minority precinct outline polygons for Chicago and Cook County taking the same steps as he did in the Florida analysis. And when the mapping was over, ArcView showed a similar result: the precincts with high concentrations of African Americans and Hispanics had some of the highest spoilage rates.

Analyzing the results in Atlanta's four counties took even more work. The *Post's* reporter downloaded the voting district file from the U.S. Census Bureau TIGER Web site and converted it into a shapefile. The counties fell under the Voting Rights Act and collected race data, but some counties provided the information on paper, others in computer format. The same was true for the election result data, so the reporter had to scan tables of data or type in data manually.

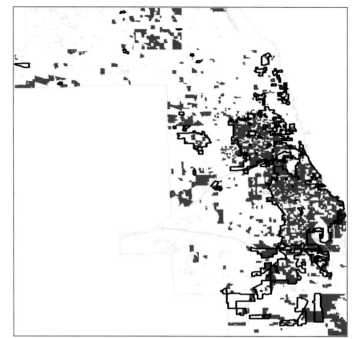

This ArcView map shows how the high minority population areas (black outline) of Chicago and Cook County line up with the precincts with a high percentage of invalidated ballots (shaded purple).

### Newsworthy findings

Though the challenges were different, the results were similar. After the reporter mapped the spoilage data and overlaid the minority voter area outlines, he could see the neighborhoods with high concentrations of minority voters had the highest spoilages rates.

The findings of the second story, which ran in late December, made it clear that the Florida results were no fluke. A political scientist quoted by the *Post* called the ballot discrepancies "disturbing and unfair," and a representative of the NAACP called for continued election reform.

National media outlets continued to follow up on the *Post's* work. That March, ABC's *Nightline* focused on the racial disparities in the Duval County ballots, mentioning some of the figures generated during the *Post's* analysis.

The coverage by the *Post* and others in the news media helped spur election reforms across the country. Florida scrapped the punch cards at the center of the showdown in the 2000 race for the White House and its counties adopted new ways of voting: computer touch screens in some counties, and optical scanners that read ovals filled in by voters in others.

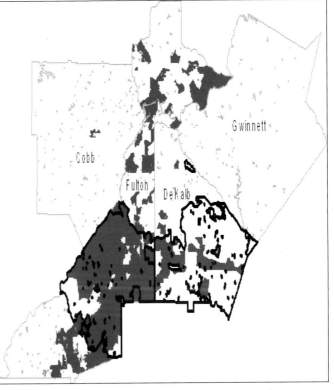

In this view of Atlanta, the black outline shows precincts where more than 50 percent of the voters were African American. The precincts shaded red had high levels of ballot invalidation. Again, the newspaper's analysis linked race and bad ballots.

## Acknowledgments

Dan Keating
Database Editor, the *Washington Post*
For providing information about the use of GIS to look for links between race and spoiled ballots, and for ArcView program screen shots.

Russell A. James,
Permissions Editor, Washington Post Writers Group
For granting permission to reprint Web graphic showing *Washington Post* newsroom.

Kim Oster
Senior Production Administrator, Washington Post Writers Group
For granting permission to reprint Web graphic showing the *Washington Post* newsroom.

# 7 *Finding homes in landslide areas*

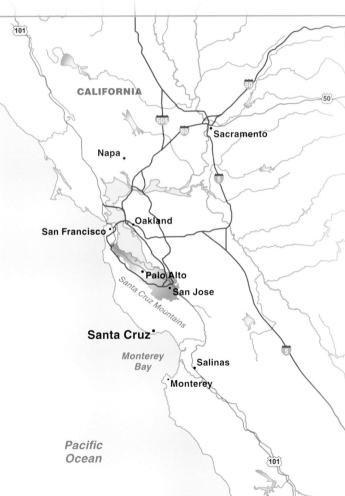

The West Coast turns into the wet coast when El Niño, a weather cycle marked by warming in the western Pacific Ocean sea surface, blows in. Torrential, unrelenting rains can soak areas that usually see low levels of rainfall. The results can be devastating. During an El Niño in 1982, rain deluged the Santa Cruz Mountains in Northern California and triggered a landslide that killed ten people. As the rain soaked the soils, the unstable land on the steep mountains ten miles north of the city of Santa Cruz gave way.

After that deadly landslide, county government authorities issued tougher building rules for people who wanted to build in the mountains. That, however, didn't slow the pace of development. Driven by the growth of software companies and new Internet ventures, the economy of the nearby Silicon Valley boomed during the 1990s. With the urban areas of the valley already settled, some homebuyers turned their eyes toward the mountains, where real estate costs were lower. Many of them poured money into their new mountain homes that had to be rigorously designed and built to meet the more stringent construction rules. In 1997, as it appeared that El Niño was on its way again, journalists at the *San Jose Mercury News* wanted to know just how many of these new homes stood in the landslide areas and in the path of danger. GIS gave them the answer.

## Using GIS and maps

Two *Mercury News* reporters got involved in the story. One of them, a computer-assisted reporting expert, knew that she could use ArcView to find the homes in landslide areas by creating a point map of the homes and overlaying that on top of a geologic layer.

First she needed to create the point map. She obtained a database from the Santa Cruz County planning department that detailed building permit information for every home that had been approved since 1985. That was when the county began computerizing its permit records, and just three years after the devastating landslide.

The database, provided on a floppy disk in a Microsoft Excel spreadsheet file, contained records for more than one thousand homes built in the mountain areas. The data included the street address of the home site, so the reporter could use the ArcView geocoding function to create a point map showing the location of each home in the mountains. Geocoding matches an address in a data table to an address range in a streets layer and creates a point that marks the location of every geocoded address.

Using the StreetMap USA extension for ArcView, the reporter was able to match more than half of the building permit locations on the first attempt by using batch processing. It turned out that some of the street names were misspelled in the permit data file, so the reporter used the interactive geocoding function to manually process a number of the addresses that had failed to match before. That got the match rate up to around 70 percent.

### Scrzprop

| Zip | Parcel | Address | City | State | |
|---|---|---|---|---|---|
| 95006.00000 | 7601202 | 320 SANTA CRUZ ST | BOULDER CREEK | CA | |
| 95006.00000 | 8110116 | 575 DAVIDSON WY | BOULDER CREEK | CA | |
| 95006.00000 | 8111601 | 13110 HAZEL AV | BOULDER CREEK | CA | |
| 95006.00000 | 8117420 | 60 E LOMOND ST | BOULDER CREEK | CA | |
| 95006.00000 | 8122119 | 12710 EAST ST | BOULDER CREEK | CA | |
| 95006.00000 | 8124110 | 12500 BOULDER ST | BOULDER CREEK | CA | |
| 95006.00000 | 8134101 | 315 HARMON ST | BOULDER CREEK | CA | |
| 95006.00000 | 8205204 | 14616 W PARK AV | BOULDER CREEK | CA | |
| 95006.00000 | 8208105 | 14300 W PARK AV | BOULDER CREEK | CA | |
| 95006.00000 | 8212401 | 14210 W PARK AV | BOULDER CREEK | CA | |
| 95006.00000 | 8218322 | 13530 DEBBY LN | BOULDER CREEK | CA | |
| 95006.00000 | 8224165 | 2000 PINECREST DR | BOULDER CREEK | CA | |
| 95006.00000 | 8228218 | 380 MIDDLETON DR | BOULDER CREEK | CA | |
| 95006.00000 | 8230224 | 832 MIDDLETON DR | BOULDER CREEK | CA | |
| 95006.00000 | 8232303 | 610 WEST RD | BOULDER CREEK | CA | |
| 95006.00000 | 8232401 | 718 MIDDLETON DR | BOULDER CREEK | CA | |
| 95006.00000 | 8233104 | 1085 MIDDLETON DR | BOULDER CREEK | CA | |
| 95006.00000 | 8234311 | 127 HILLSIDE AV | BOULDER CREEK | CA | |
| 95006.00000 | 8235110 | 14785 BIG BASIN HWY | BOULDER CREEK | CA | |
| 95006.00000 | 8312127 | 178 MADRONA RD | BOULDER CREEK | CA | |
| 95006.00000 | 8316115 | 15220 BIG BASIN HWY | BOULDER CREEK | CA | |
| 95006.00000 | 8322207 | 331 ACORN DR | BOULDER CREEK | CA | |
| 95006.00000 | 8323223 | 124 ASPEN LN | BOULDER CREEK | CA | |
| 95006.00000 | 8326136 | 500 N SPRING CREEK RD | BOULDER CREEK | CA | |

Santa Cruz County planners provided the *Mercury News* with a data file listing every building permit issued since 1985—when the records first were computerized. The file listed the parcel number, street address, and other location information for each property. Boulder Creek is one of the Santa Cruz County communities included in the analysis.

Another problem she encountered was that some of the roads in the streets address field of the building permits table had only recently been built and were not yet in the streets file. So she went out to the sites in the mountains to make sure that the addresses existed. If the addresses existed, she checked to see whether she could use a nearby address for each or an intersection to plot an approximate location. Although some of the addresses could not be mapped, the reporter concluded that the *Mercury News* had matched enough addresses to perform the analysis.

The reporter needed a geologic layer for the county that showed, among other things, potential landslide areas. She obtained one from someone she knew at the U.S. Geological Survey through a local GIS users' group. (GIS software users sometimes form users groups to share information.) The U.S. Geological Survey used ArcInfo and provided the file in ArcInfo Export format. The reporter converted the file to a shapefile using the Import71 utility that came with her copy of ArcView 3.2. All she needed to do was specify the computer directory path and file name of the Export file and the same for the shape-file she wanted to create.

Geocoding turned the building permits address data file into a geocoded table that ArcView could display as points on a map. Note that the first column of the geocoded table specifies that these records have point locations assigned.

A local U.S. Geological Survey representative gave the *Mercury News* a geologic layer for Santa Cruz County in ArcInfo Export format. The reporter converted it to a shapefile using a utility that came with ArcView. The GIS user specifies the path and name of the export file in the utility's interface, and also specifies the path and name of the output shapefile.

## Symbolizing data

After importing the polygon file, she added it to her view. Without symbolizing the data, it didn't provide much information. The reporter chose to symbolize the data based on a numeric code that indicated the potential for a landslide. Using the Legend Editor, she symbolized the layer using that field to show the areas with the highest risk.

The two layers failed to line up properly in her view because the county geologic layer was projected and the point file was not. Projections are used to represent geographical information about the three-dimensional earth on two-dimensional maps. Some projections aim to protect the accuracy of distance, while others aim to protect the accuracy of areas and shapes.

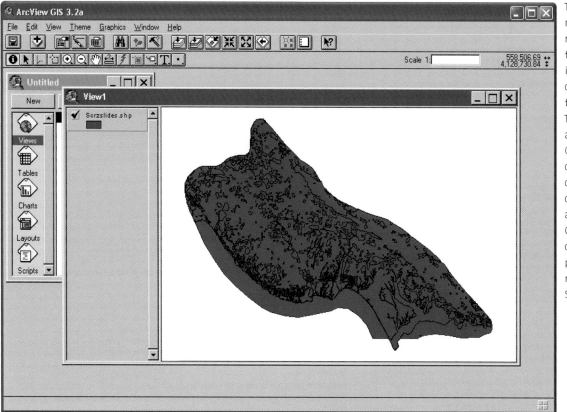

The *Mercury News* reporter opened the new shapefile in ArcView for the first time and it appeared as one color, with dark lines for polygon borders. The shapefile included a data field called Lsct (short for landslide category), which contained five possible codes for the land type assigned by the U.S. Geological Survey. One code identified areas prone to landslides. The map layer shows all of Santa Cruz County.

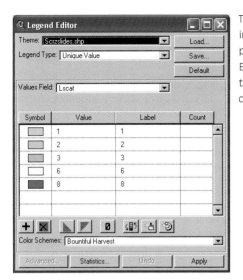

The reporter double-clicked the theme's legend in the Table of Contents on the right side of the program window to activate the theme's Legend Editor. She created a Unique Value map to display the values contained in the Lscat field as a unique color symbol (on the left of the grid).

The resulting map displayed the geologic categories. Category 8, shown as dark brown, represents the areas that were mostly landslides. Category 1 represents lands that were not categorized, Category 2 represents water, Category 3 represents flat land with surface deposits, and Category 6 represents areas with few or no mapped landslides.

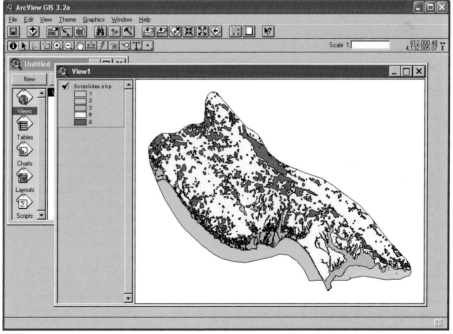

### Using the extension

The reporter had to project the points layer into the same projection as the geologic layer. She used the Projector! extension that came with her version of ArcView to do that. After opening the extensions box using the File\Extensions menu item, she checked the box for the Projector! Utility. That added a button to launch the program.

With the building permit point file open, she clicked on the Projector! button to run the program.

She had to project the point layer into the projection used by the U.S. Geological Survey for the geologic layer: Universal Transverse Mercator, zone 10, in meters using surveying points for North America that were established in 1927. (This measurement system is called NAD 1927).

First she selected meters as the type of output units. Next she selected a projection category of UTM–1927 and the Type as Zone 10.

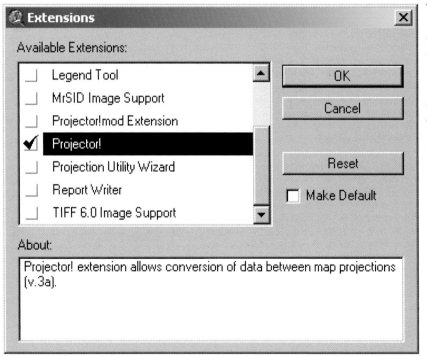

The point file displaying the locations of the new homes was unprojected and had to be projected to match the Santa Cruz County geologic layer. The Santa Cruz County layer had been provided by the U.S. Geological Survey in the Universal Transverse Mercator (UTM) Zone 10 projection, using meters and North American measurement points established in 1927. To project the point layer, the reporter used the Projector! extension. She added the Projector! extension in ArcView through the Files\Extensions menu item and checked the proper box.

Projector! added a button to ArcView to launch the extension.

First the reporter had to set the output units for the projected layer. She chose meters to match the units in the geologic map.

**Projector!**

Please pick output units

meters

OK

Cancel

**Projection Properties**

◉ Standard   ○ Custom

OK

Cancel

Category: Projections of the World

Type: Geographic

Projection: Geographic

Then she had to set the Category and Type of projection using this window.

**Projection Properties**

◉ Standard   ○ Custom

OK

Cancel

Category: UTM - 1927

Type: Zone 10

Projection: Transverse Mercator

Spheroid: Clarke 1866

Central Meridian: -123

Reference Latitude: 0

Scale Factor: 0.9996

False Easting: 500000

False Northing: 0

She selected UTM–1927 for the Category and Zone 10 for the Type. Both of these selections mirrored the settings for the geologic layer.

### Reaching conclusions

Now it was time to figure out which of those homes were inside the landslide areas. For that, the reporter used the ArcView Select by Theme function. The Select by Theme function allows users to select features in one layer based upon their proximity to features in another layer.

Performing the selection took a few steps. First, she used the ArcView Query Builder tool by clicking its button. Once it was open she queried the geologic layer's landslide category field, to select only the areas with mostly landslides. Next, she overlaid the point layer displaying the locations where building permits had been issued and made that theme active.

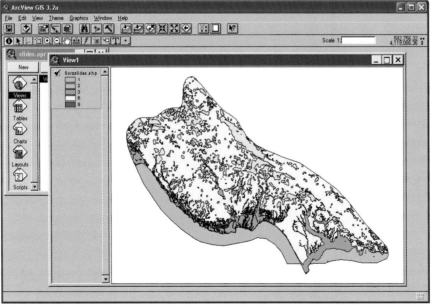

Using the ArcView Query Builder tool, the reporter created a query that selected only the areas with a landslide category of 8 (for mostly landslides).

The mostly landslide areas were selected in the map view, highlighted in yellow.

Last, she used the Select by Theme function. In the selection dialog box, she instructed ArcView to select the building points that intersected the selected features of the geologic layer (the mostly landslides areas). ArcView selected the locations, highlighting the selected purple points as yellow. The reporter could see the homes that stood in harm's way.

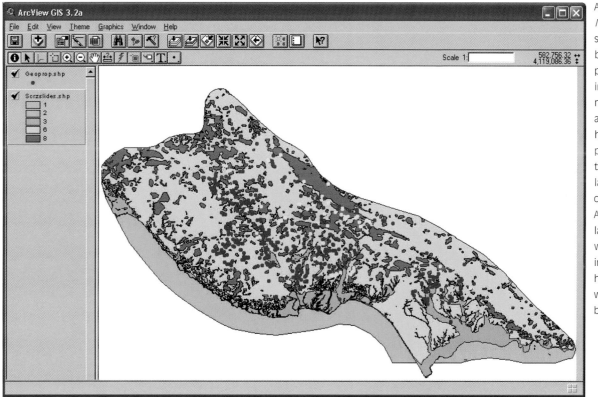

After the *Mercury News* reporter selected the building permit points that intersected the mostly landslide areas, ArcView highlighted the purple points from the Geoprop.shp layer in yellow on the map. After the mostly landslides areas were unselected in ArcView, the highlighted points were shown as bright yellow dots.

## Informing readers

Hundreds of new homes, it turned out, were built in mountain areas that were prone to landslides. The reporters' story, which ran in early 1998, detailed the growth of homes inside the potential landslide areas. The story included a link to landslide and mudslide maps that the U.S. Geological Survey posted on the Web at *elnino.usgs.gov/landslides-sfbay*. A map showing the landslide areas and housing permits accompanied the story (next page).

The story made readers aware of the potential landslide dangers. Some reacted to the story by calling the *Mercury News* newsroom and saying they were worried that they might be in danger. A couple of big developers also called to thank the newspaper for the story.

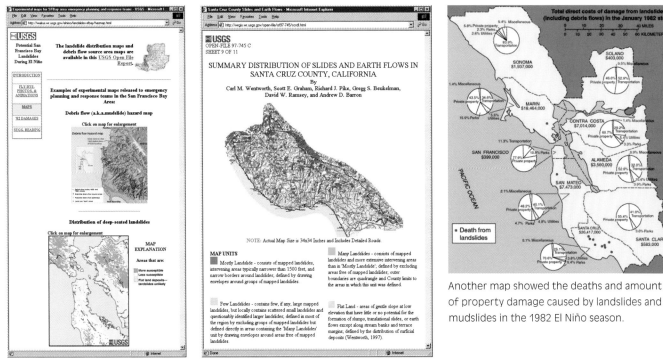

The *Mercury News* article included a link to the U.S. Geological Survey's San Francisco Bay area landslide page, where readers could view more maps.

One of the maps on the U.S. Geological Survey displayed the landslide zones and other geologic features.

Another map showed the deaths and amount of property damage caused by landslides and mudslides in the 1982 El Niño season.

# San Jose Mercury News

FINAL EDITION FC
$1.50

*Serving Northern California Since 1851*

W W W . M E R C U R Y C E N T E R . C O M

SUNDAY
.... JANUARY 11, 1998

## Slippery slope of disregard

■ **Boom:** Hundreds build in landslide areas on the faith engineering will save them.

BY JOHN WOOLFOLK AND JENNIFER LaFLEUR
Mercury News Staff Writers

Since the disastrous Santa Cruz Mountains mudslides of January 1982, hundreds of new homes have been built in mountainous areas that geologists have identified as landslide-prone, a Mercury News analysis of county building permits and federal geologic maps shows.

Boom times in Silicon Valley have brought home buyers who can afford to build gravity-defying aeries in the Santa Cruz Mountains and are willing to hire the engineers to create them.

"More and more people are building large, elaborate houses in marginal areas," said Gerald Weber, a consulting geologist and professor at the University of California-Santa Cruz. "Some of those will have severe problems during exceedingly wet years."

Safety requirements for construction are tougher than ever. But geologists say civilization is pushing into more precarious areas and that if El Niño forecasts hold true for record rainfall like the downpours that
See **MUDSLIDES**, *Back Page*

The *Mercury News'* coverage was enhanced by maps and drawings that showed landslide areas and explained dangerous conditions. GIS played a key role in helping to develop, analyze, and present the information to readers.

## Unstable slopes pose slide threat

Heavy rains in the winters of 1981-82 and 1982-83 caused devastating landslides in the hills of Santa Cruz County. More disasters could happen because new homes have been built in potential slide areas. Scientists with the U.S. Geological Survey have surveyed the hills for two kinds of slide hazards: slow-moving landslides and rapid — sometimes deadly — debris flows.

### Slow-moving landslides

Geologists identified slow-moving landslides through ground and aerial surveys. The red areas are mostly covered with landslides. The purple squares, which are not to scale, identify where building permits have been issued for new homes in mountain areas of Santa Cruz County since 1985.

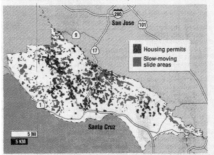

These slides involve a layer of rock from 10 feet to several hundred feet deep overlying another, less permeable rock layer. Water seeping through the upper layer pushes the layers apart, allowing the upper layer to slide downhill. Because water takes a long time to seep below the rock, slides can occur months after the rainfall.

### Rapid debris flows

If it rains hard enough, rapid debris flows can occur on any slopes of at least 20 degrees, regardless of soil type, said USGS geologist David Howell. Geologists used a computer program to identify these slopes based on digitized data from topographic maps, shown below in pink.

In this case, a layer of thin, loose soil six inches to a few yards deep is on top of less permeable rock. Heavy rains — at least six to 10 inches in a day in the Santa Cruz Mountains and four to six inches in the East Bay hills — turn the soil into a muddy fluid that spills down the hill, picking up more mud, trees and other objects as it goes, moving at 10 to 20 mph. Debris flows have been known to reach 100 mph.

The U.S. Geological Survey will have landslide maps available online at the end of January at: **elnino.usgs.gov/landslides-sfbay**
Sources: David Howell, U.S. Geological Survey, Menlo Park; Mercury News analysis of Santa Cruz County building permits

REID BROWN, CARL NEIBURGER AND JENNIFER LAFLEUR — MERCURY NEWS

## Acknowledgments

Jennifer LaFleur
McCormick Tribune Journalism Fellow, Reporters Committee for Freedom of the Press and formerly of the *San Jose Mercury News*
For information about the use of GIS to locate homes in landslide areas, and for providing a copy of the resulting newspaper article and ArcView program screen shots.

Rich Ramirez
Assistant to the Executive Editor, *San Jose Mercury News*
For providing permission to reproduce the newspaper article.

# 8 *Zeroing in on environmental hazards*

Poor Americans who live in public housing projects often have crime, rundown buildings, and a host of social ills as neighbors. Find a public housing project, and there's a chance it's smack in the middle of the worst part of town. For many of the residents, whose monthly rental payments are covered in part by federal subsidies, there sometimes is no way out. Making matters worse, residents of public housing projects often are forced to live near old dumps or industrial plants whose smokestacks pump toxic fumes into the air.

During the past couple of decades, activists in pursuit of "environmental justice" have been fighting environmental threats to poor people—many of them minorities. Journalists have followed suit by scrutinizing plans to place dumps, waste incinerators, and other potential health threats near poor neighborhoods. In some cases, GIS has played a major role in that effort, including a noteworthy example in Texas.

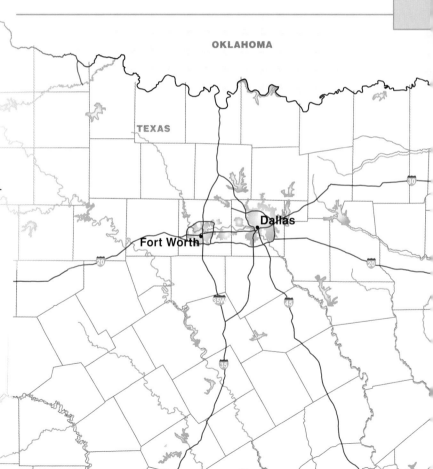

### Efforts in Texas

In 1993, two *Dallas Morning News* reporters examined a government plan to use taxpayer money to renovate a sprawling, thirty-five-hundred-unit public housing project in west Dallas that was near a shuttered lead smelter. Workers there had reclaimed lead from dead vehicle batteries. Even though the smelter had been inactive for seven years, lead that had spewed from its stacks still contaminated the neighborhood soil.

The nine-month investigation found that the plan would have forced thousands of African-American families to live in the neighborhood, which was on a government list of potential Superfund toxic sites. After the newspaper's "Race and Risk" series ran, the U.S. secretary of Housing and Urban Development killed the renovation project and granted vouchers to the families remaining in the project so they could find rental housing elsewhere in Dallas.

After the series ran, the reporters also started thinking: If U.S. Housing and Urban Development officials had decided to allow the west Dallas public housing project next to an environmental hazard, HUD probably had approved placing public housing projects near toxic sites all across the United States.

Anecdotally, the reporters knew that HUD had allowed public housing projects near toxic threats. They knew about suits filed against the government by public housing residents who claimed that HUD, local housing agencies, and private developers had exposed them to environmental hazards. It was a hot local story in some areas, but no newspaper had examined the proximity of environmental hazards to public housing residents on a national scale. The reporters decided to take on the project, and GIS helped them report on some of the worst areas.

The newspaper's environmental reporter, who had worked on "Race and Risk," was familiar with GIS. He had used GIS only a little, but knew about how environmental researchers used it. The newsroom lacked a GIS program and expertise, so it turned to outside help.

The *Morning News* hired the Bruton Center for Development Studies in the School of Social Sciences at the University of Texas at Dallas. The center specializes in using GIS to conduct social research. Another reporter—one of three working on the stories—had known about the center from his previous reporting.

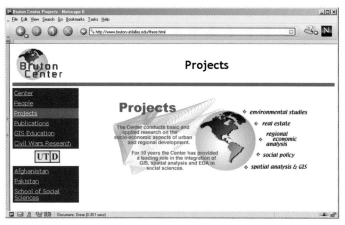

The *Dallas Morning News* contracted with the Bruton Center for Development Studies at the University of Texas at Dallas to conduct the spatial analysis of public housing projects and environmental hazards.

### Identifying data

Around 1996, the reporters spoke with the director of the Bruton Center and filled him in on what they wanted to accomplish with their reporting project and the public policy issues involved, without revealing what the reporters already had found. The reporters wanted to ensure that the research center's work would stand free of influence. The researchers at the center advised the reporters on the technical aspects of obtaining data for GIS analysis.

Then the reporters started identifying the data they needed for the story. First, for the GIS analysis, they needed a file with the identity and location of every public housing project in the country. Then they needed data for environmental risks. They decided to seek national data that had the location of every facility emitting toxic substances. Environmental regulators that the reporters interviewed said that the air emissions posed the most immediate threat to human health, so the reporters decided to focus on air polluters. Also, they decided to seek data about every hazardous waste site in the United States.

Federal regulators readily provided the environmental data to the reporters at no cost. The reporters got two databases from the Environmental Protection Agency. One was the Toxic Release Inventory (TRI), which has information about industrial facilities that emit potentially harmful materials into the air, water, or ground. The TRI identifies the substance released and the amount. It also includes the facility's longitude and latitude, as reported by the facility owner.

Reporters for the *Morning News* obtained Toxic Release Inventory (TRI) data from the U.S. Environmental Protection Agency (EPA). The TRI data contains information about facilities that pollute the air. The EPA now makes the data available for download on the Web.

The Toxic Release Inventory data, shown here in a Microsoft Access table, includes the names of polluting facilities, addresses, and chemicals released. It also includes the longitudes and latitudes, which can be mapped to create a point shapefile.

The newspaper also received the Comprehensive Environmental Response, Compensation, and Liability Information System (CERCLIS) database of hazardous waste sites, which also had longitude and latitude reported. These longitude and latitude readings were more accurate, because the EPA had obtained them itself.

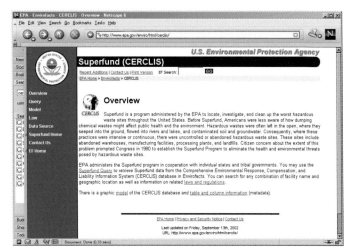

Comprehensive Environmental Response, Compensation, and Liability Information System (CERCLIS) data is available from the federal Environmental Protection Agency. The CERCLIS data lists every known hazardous waste site in the United States. The EPA also makes this data available for download on the Web.

The CERCLIS data, shown in this Microsoft Access table, includes the name of the hazardous waste site and the latitude and longitude coordinates. A GIS program, such as ArcView, can create a point shapefile from the coordinates.

## Demanding information

Getting a database of the public housing projects, along with demographic data, and latitude and longitude proved much more difficult. Responding to the reporters' initial request, HUD officials denied that they even had the data, possibly out of ignorance. But the reporters knew otherwise—they even knew the name of the database—and filed a federal Freedom of Information Act request to obtain it.

Early on in the reporting and analysis, the reporters and researchers had to cobble together a less comprehensive database out of two smaller HUD data files that contained information about housing projects, including the longitude and latitude coordinates. That allowed them to start working on the analysis.

(A few years later, HUD provided more detailed and complete data from 1998 for the public housing projects, including longitude and latitude coordinates.)

The U.S. Department of Housing and Urban Development provided the *Morning News* with a copy of its database listing the location of every public housing project in the country. The database, called A Picture of Subsidized Households, is now available on the Web.

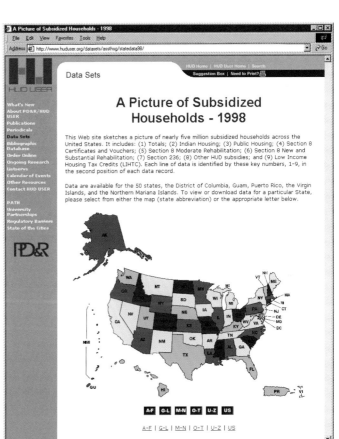

The data lists each public housing project, as seen in this Microsoft Access table (below). It includes the latitude and longitude for every project. An ArcView user can turn this into a point map using the Add Event Theme function.

| LAT | LONG | PGM | NAME | CODE | UNITS |
|---|---|---|---|---|---|
| 45.513 | -122.866 | 67 | Aloha Park | OR_12644172 | 8l |
| 45.493 | -122.857 | 67 | West Park Terrace | OR_12644115 | 3 |
| 45.479 | -122.862 | 66 | Devonshire Manor | OR160044001 | 2l |
| 45.487 | -122.84 | 66 | Farmington Meadows | OR16H029150 | 6l |
| 45.488 | -122.865 | 66 | uAloha Projec | OR16T821010 | 1l |

## More questions

With the data in hand, the reporters returned to the Bruton Center. They also had a list of roughly a dozen questions for the GIS researchers: What percent of public housing projects reside within one mile of a facility that emits toxics into the air or a hazardous waste site? What percentage of housing projects whose residents are mostly minorities are within one mile? What percentage of housing projects whose residents are mostly white are within one mile?

Most environmental justice studies select hazards and examine the surrounding populations. What the *Morning News* reporters wanted to do was just the opposite: Select the public housing projects and see what hazards surrounded them. The *Morning News* included only those projects that had at least twenty-five units, so the focus would be on the ones with the greatest potential risks. The GIS specialists at the Bruton Center got to work.

Early in the reporting, back in 1996, the center used ArcInfo, a high-end GIS program from ESRI to select public housing projects that had a toxic waste site within one mile. The analysis found that 30 percent of the projects were within a mile of a toxic waste site. The center repeated the analysis for projects and air polluters. (For more technical details about the hazardous waste site-housing project analysis, visit *www.bruton.utdallas.edu/educ/prj_students/dlauder/gisproj.html*.)

Two years later the center performed a second round of analysis for housing project proximity to the air polluters. Working with fresh data from the EPA and HUD, the center created its own program and ran spatial calculations based on the proximity to an air polluter, the amount of the chemical emitted, and the potency. The center ranked the results and generated a list of the worst public housing project locations.

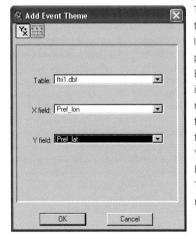

The researchers turned the Toxic Release Inventory data into points by using the Add Event Theme function in ArcView. First the researchers identified the TRI table, and then they selected the X and Y fields to define the longitude and latitude. Then they saved the results as a shapefile.

Once the Toxic Release Inventory data was imported to ArcView, the researchers could look at it in the table view. Each record in the database listed a facility and its latitude and longitude.

## Mapping with software

Looking at the air pollution results, the reporters knew that they wanted to focus on the Alameda Corridor of central Los Angeles, home to heavy industry and several large public housing projects. So the researchers at the Bruton Center mapped the air polluters and the housing projects using ArcView. The researchers manually created polygon shapefiles that displayed the boundaries of the housing projects. Then they used the Add Event Theme function to translate the latitude and longitude coordinates in the Toxic Release data file into points on the map.

Once the Bruton Center researchers had those two in the view and added other features, they printed the map for the reporters. Looking at the map, the reporters easily could see the concentrations of environmental hazards around public housing projects. Graphic artists at the *Morning News* took a printed GIS map of the corridor and used it to create a map of the area that ran in the newspaper.

The reporters earlier had decided against mapping the hazardous waste sites in the map because environmental researchers had told them that the air polluters posed a more immediate health threat to the people living nearby.

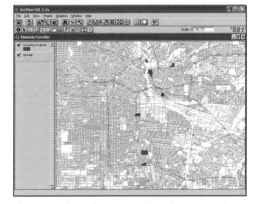

The researchers first created a polygon map layer that displayed the locations of public housing projects in the Alameda Corridor of central Los Angeles. This map shows the public housing in the heavily industrialized corridor.

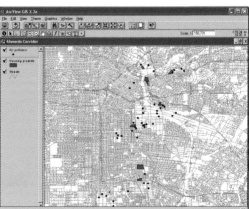

The researchers then overlaid the TRI data shapefile; that displayed all the polluters near the public housing projects. The image below shows a zoomed view of one of the housing projects and nearby polluters.

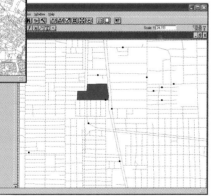

On October 1, 2000, the *Dallas Morning News* ran its "Toxic Neighbors" story, the first in its "Toxic Traps" series. A map that accompanied the story, showing the geographic relationships of housing projects and toxics sources in Los Angeles' Alameda Corridor, is a good example of how GIS maps help graphic artists develop print maps for publication in the newspaper.

# The Dallas Morning News

"We are exposing children from their earliest years to asthma and respiratory problems and skin problems. But we sweep it under the rug and forget about it."

— *Henry Cisneros, former HUD secretary*

# TOXIC NEIGHBORS

The Carver Terrace project was built near refineries in Port Arthur, Texas, in the 1950s. Residents blame health problems on pollution.

## Residents of projects find common problem: Pollution

*Public housing and pollution*

**TOXIC TRAPS**

*First in a series*

Staff story by
**Craig Flournoy**
and **Randy Lee Loftis**

Staff photography by
**David Woo**

Decisions by federal and local officials have forced nearly 1 million American families to live in polluted neighborhoods at taxpayer expense.

The people are disproportionately minority and are all crushingly poor. Many had to wait years to get out of falling-down, firetrap slums and into apartments where federal money helps pay the rent.

What they didn't know was that in cities across the country, public housing that should have been a godsend was instead a toxic trap.

In Los Angeles and Chicago, Chester, Pa., and Port Arthur, Texas, public housing is in the same neighborhoods with factories that pour toxic pollution into the air. In New Orleans and Bossier City, La., it is next door to land where toxic waste was dumped for decades. In Jacksonville, Fla., and Daly City, Calif., it was built right on top of toxic waste.

In a nationwide look at government-subsidized housing, *The Dallas Morning News* found scores of such problems.

In every case, local officials or developers chose the sites and federal officials approved them — often decades before scientists fully understood the

potential health risks.

Public health researchers know a lot more today. They have linked proximity to toxic air pollution and toxic waste sites to health risks ranging from cancer to birth defects. But thousands of families continue to live in public housing in polluted neighborhoods — and the federal government has committed more

than $4 billion since 1993 to rebuild public housing in many of those same places.

The U.S. Department of Housing and Urban Development funds and oversees subsidized housing. A spokesman said in a written statement that the agency is not

**Please see RESEARCHERS on Page 22A.**

Candace Bell regularly uses a nebulizer for asthma that began after her family moved to Altgeld Gardens, a decaying housing project in Chicago.

The highly industrialized Alameda Corridor. **23A**
Refinery accidents raise fears among residents. **24A**

**DallasNews.com/EXTRA**
TOXIC TRAPS: Swipe here to find out if there are EPA sites near your home. Also on the Web: additional articles and photos.

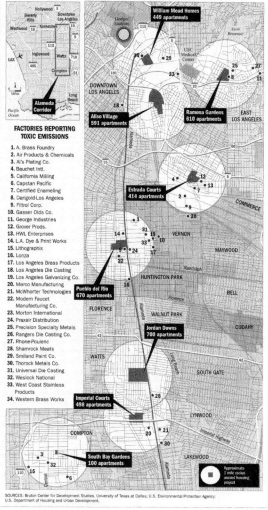

## THE ALAMEDA CORRIDOR

The map below shows the location of eight public housing projects along the Alameda Corridor in Los Angeles as well as 34 factories that reported toxic air emissions to the U.S. Environmental Protection Agency in 1997. Each factory is located within approximately one mile of one or more of the public housing projects. The eight projects include some 4,000 apartments.

### FACTORIES REPORTING TOXIC EMISSIONS

1. A. Brass Foundry
2. Air Products & Chemicals
3. Al's Plating Co.
4. Bauchet Intl.
5. California Milling
6. Capstan Pacific
7. Certified Enameling
8. Darigold-Los Angeles
9. Filtrol Corp.
10. Gasser Olds Co.
11. George Industries
12. Grover Prods.
13. HWL Enterprises
14. L.A. Dye & Print Works
15. Lithographix
16. Lonza
17. Los Angeles Brass Products
18. Los Angeles Die Casting
19. Los Angeles Galvanizing Co.
20. Marco Manufacturing
21. McWhorter Technologies
22. Modern Faucet Manufacturing Co.
23. Morton International
24. Praxair Distribution
25. Precision Specialty Metals
26. Rangers Die Casting Co.
27. Rhone-Poulenc
28. Shamrock Meats
29. Smiland Paint Co.
30. Thorock Metals Co.
31. Universal Die Casting
32. Weslock National
33. West Coast Stainless Products
34. Western Brass Works

**William Mead Homes** 449 apartments
**Aliso Village** 591 apartments
**Ramona Gardens** 610 apartments
**Estrada Courts** 414 apartments
**Pueblo del Rio** 670 apartments
**Jordan Downs** 700 apartments
**Imperial Courts** 498 apartments
**South Bay Gardens** 100 apartments

Approximate 1 mile radius around housing project

SOURCES: Bruton Center for Development Studies, University of Texas at Dallas; U.S. Environmental Protection Agency; U.S. Department of Housing and Urban Development.

*The Dallas Morning News*

## Telling conclusions

In its main story, the *Morning News* reported that almost one-half of all the U.S. public housing projects, home to 870,000 families, were within one mile of an air polluter. In addition, 40 percent of all U.S. public housing projects were within one mile of a toxic waste site.

The newspaper also reported that half of the mostly minority projects had a toxic factory nearby while only one-third of the mostly white projects did. Those findings gave the *Morning News* the backbone of its three-day series, called "Toxic Traps."

The *Morning News* and its Web site's parent company hired a contractor that created an interactive address search tool that accompanied the "Toxic Traps" series on the Web. Users filled in a form containing spots for their home address and a distance then clicked to get a list of all the air polluters and toxic dumps within that specified distance. The users could then click a link for each air polluter or dump and get more specific information. Users also could get a map of the vicinity. Another part of the Web site listed the U.S. public housing projects, with each linked to specific information about the nearby environmental hazards.

A few weeks before the *Morning News* series ran, the U.S. Department of Housing and Urban Development launched its E-Maps service on the Web *(www.hud.gov/offices/cio/emaps/index/cfm)*. The service, powered by ArcIMS, lets users zoom in on a geographic area and see environmental hazards identified by the Environmental Protection Agency. The service also includes the locations of public housing projects.

## Interactive search tool

Just weeks before the series ran, HUD unveiled its E-Maps service on its Web site that allowed users to map the proximity of environmental hazards to public housing with an ArcIMS application. ArcIMS is a program that serves interactive maps—using standard shapefiles—over the Internet.

The day the series began in the *Morning News,* HUD issued a news release that criticized the newspaper's story and said it unfairly accused the agency of environmental racism based upon the proximity of "a mere handful" of housing projects to polluters. HUD said that it conducts thorough environmental reviews of new project sites selected by local government officials and then orders the remediation of any identified hazards.

In the weeks after the series ran, the newspaper's interactive Web site attracted increased traffic. Later, the package won a 2001 EPpy Award—given out by *Editor & Publisher* magazine—for the best special section in a newspaper online service.

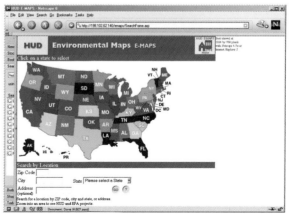

99

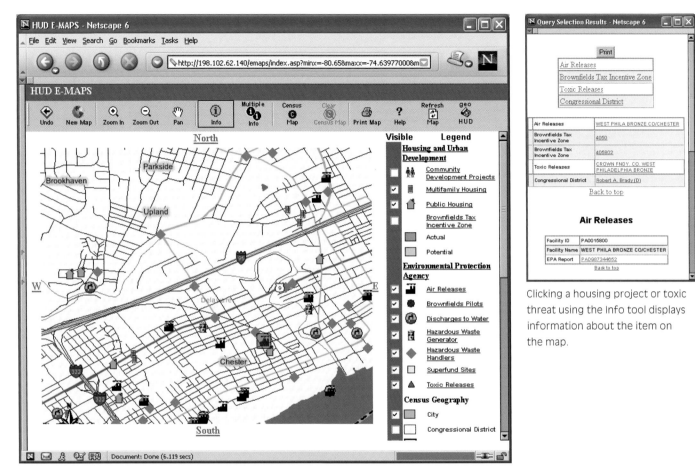

This HUD E-Maps image shows public housing and toxic sites in Chester, Pennsylvania, one of the cities examined in the "Toxic Traps" series. The map displays the locations of public housing projects (the green house symbols) and a variety of toxic threats.

Clicking a housing project or toxic threat using the Info tool displays information about the item on the map.

## Acknowledgments

Randy Loftis
Reporter, the *Dallas Morning News*
For providing information about the use of GIS in reporting the "Toxic Traps" series, and for a reprint of the series.

Craig Flournoy
Assistant Professor, Southern Methodist University, and former *Dallas Morning News* reporter
For providing information about the use of GIS in reporting the "Toxic Traps" series.

John Cranfill
Senior Editor, Belo Interactive
For providing information about the use of interactive tools on the "Toxic Traps" series Web pages.

Stuart Wilk
Vice President and Managing Editor, the *Dallas Morning News*
For granting permission to reprint graphics showing parts of the "Toxic Traps" series.

James C. Murdoch
Dean, School of Social Sciences at University of Texas at Dallas and former director of the Bruton Center
For providing information about the use of GIS in reporting the "Toxic Traps series," ArcView data, and program screen shots.

Paul Jargowsky
Associate Professor, University of Texas at Dallas, and director of the Bruton Center
For granting permission to reprint Bruton Center Web page.

Paul A. Waddell
Associate Professor, University of Washington, and former director of the Bruton Center
For providing information about the use of GIS in reporting the "Toxic Traps" series.

# 9 *Uncovering inequitable assessments*

Local governments and school districts across the country raise a large share of their operating funds through real estate taxes. Each year, property owners are taxed based on simple math: the value of their property times the local tax rate, as set by local legislators and school boards. The higher the value of a property, the higher its tax bill. Similar properties are supposed to have similar assessed values. Even though government officials and agencies establish formulas, procedures, and systems to try to ensure equity, owners frequently appeal what they believe are unfair assessments.

At the *Columbus Dispatch,* a reporter wanted to dig deeper into residential property tax equity in the city and surrounding Franklin County, Ohio. He used GIS to discover unequal tax burdens, something no one else in the county had done before.

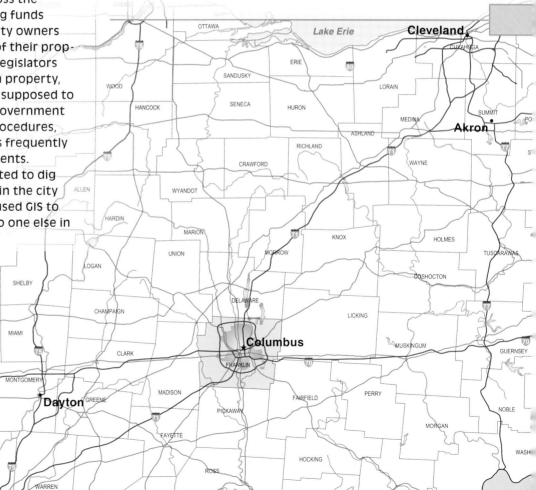

### The background

In typical jurisdictions, a local government official called the tax assessor sets the property value, often using a complex formula that takes into account all kinds of factors. For residential properties, that may mean property type, number of bedrooms, lot size, finished square footage, and dozens of other features. In spite of all of those variables, tax assessors are supposed to ensure that similar properties have similar assessed values. A property owner who believes the assessor has set the value of his property too high may challenge the assessment before a hearing board.

Many states by law monitor the overall accuracy of property assessments by conducting studies that compare the assessed values of recently sold properties to the sale prices. The closer the assessed value to the sale price, the more accurate the assessment. If a state finds a wide disparity between the overall sale prices and the assessed values, it orders the local government agency or school board to adjust—or "equalize"—overall assessed values by a certain percentage.

Those studies provide a snapshot of overall assessment accuracy without taking a more detailed picture that can reveal whether certain neighborhoods shoulder an unequal tax burden, or whether owners of high-end properties, relatively speaking, have lower levels of assessment than owners of low-cost properties.

At the *Dispatch*, a reporter knew from earlier reporting in Springfield, Illinois, that low-income neighborhoods often have higher assessment burdens than upper-income neighborhoods. In other words, the homes in low-income neighborhoods tend to have assessed values that are greater than their market values, as measured by their sales prices. The opposite tends to be true in upper-income neighborhoods.

Since he wasn't using GIS at the time he was working in Springfield (this had been in the early 1990s), he tackled the reporting project the old-fashioned way: with a paper map, colored markers, and pins.

Over a few months, while working on other stories, he used the pins and markers to display assessment information for recently sold properties on the map of assessment areas. When he finished recording the information for some 300 properties, he saw an unmistakable pattern. Areas in the east, which were predominantly lower-income and African American, had a larger percentage of overassessed properties. Areas in the west, which were predominantly upper-income and white, had a larger percentage of under-assessed properties.

He had a story: Homeowners in poor, African-American neighborhoods shouldered a greater tax burden than their counterparts in upper-income, white neighborhoods.

## Hunting down data

After he took a reporting job at the *Columbus Dispatch*, the reporter decided to look at the assessments there. He started laying the groundwork by requesting assessment data from the Franklin County Auditor's office, the government agency responsible for performing the property assessments. The auditor's office responded that the data was available on nine-track tapes in EBCDIC, an IBM® mainframe format. Many journalists who have obtained data on nine-track tapes have found the process of downloading the data to a format that a PC can understand painstaking and often fraught with error.

When the reporter for the *Dispatch* eventually got the data, it turned out the tapes were defective and could not be downloaded properly. Later, the reporter learned elsewhere that the auditor's office had put the same assessment data onto a CD–ROM—something that was much easier to use than nine-track tapes. So nine months later the newspaper requested the CD with the data stored in dBASE tables. The newspaper paid less than $25 for the data. The data included a number of fields of information, such as sale price, assessment, and sale date.

The database itself was complex, with around twenty tables that were linked by a common fourteen-character identification number. The *Dispatch* reporter needed additional data about property transactions between unaffiliated parties from the state of Ohio, so he got that and merged it with auditor data using Microsoft Access.

The *Dispatch's* reporter requested data from the Franklin County Auditor, the government office that assesses properties for tax purposes. Initially the office provided the data on nine-track tape in IBM EBCDIC format.

Journalists downloading data from nine-track tape onto a PC can use software designed for the task. Still, the process is arduous and loaded with the possibility for error. ReelView II, a program that was developed by two journalists, allows users to view raw data on the tape before transferring it.

The *Dispatch* reporter merged auditor data and data from the state into one master table containing information about property assessed values and sales. He merged the data in Microsoft Access database manager. The table contained year of sale, sale price, and other data.

### Discovering GIS

Around the same time the reporter obtained the data from the county auditor, he and a *Dispatch* editor saw an ArcView demonstration at a reporters conference, where an idea struck him: A GIS program is just like a database manager with a map; a GIS can query data and show the results on a map or in a table.

Shortly after that conference, the *Dispatch* newsroom bought ArcView and the reporter started to use it for the property tax story.

With the assessment data and GIS program in hand, the reporter needed to obtain the map layer files for the analysis. He got those in ArcView format from the Franklin County Development Department's Web site. The parcel files also included the unique fourteen-digit identification number for each parcel.

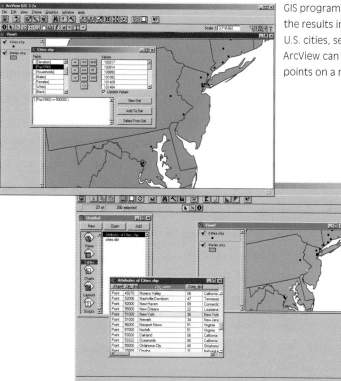

GIS programs can query data like a database manager and display the results in a table or on a map. Here the user queries data about U.S. cities, selecting those with a population greater than 500,000. ArcView can display the selected cities as records in a data table or points on a map.

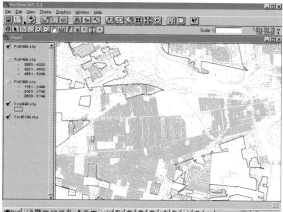

The *Dispatch* obtained ArcView map files from the county Department of Planning and Building. The map files allowed the display of each parcel of real estate as a polygon or point. This view shows the residential properties as blue points on the west side of Columbus.

## Using GIS

The GIS work was relatively simple. The reporter chose to work with a point shapefile, with a point representing each residential parcel in the county. He simply joined the assessor data to the map layer by performing these steps:

First, he created a new ArcView project and added the point layer to the empty display.

Then he added the dBASE table with the assessment data for every parcel. He opened the dBASE table to view its data, and then did the same for the map layer file.

Finally, he joined the assessment data to the map by clicking the identification number field header in the assessment data table and the identification number field header in the map table. Then he clicked the Join Tables button.

The reporter had to open two tables in ArcView to display data for the residential properties as color-coded points on the map. One was a dBASE data table (right) that contained sales and value information. Another was the table for the residential property points (left).

He attached the data to the properties map point table by clicking the common field in each (the fourteen-digit identifier) and then performing a join. The blue bar at the bottom of the ArcView program window shows the progress of the join.

That prepared the data for mapping. The reporter chose to display the points for each parcel based on whether the parcel was assessed too high (more than 10 percent above the sale price) or too low (less than 10 percent below the sale price). Using the Legend Editor in the Table of Contents, he symbolized the high assessments as red dots and the low assessments as green dots. In addition, he showed variations in the over- and underassessments by graduating the shades of the green and red dots. The deeper the shade, the greater the over- or underassessment.

With the help of an editor, the reporter then layered income and demographic data from the 1990 Census under the dots.

It was difficult to see all the dots for nine years of sales, so the reporter mapped the data year by year from 1992 through 2000 and got consistent results: Properties in upper-income neighborhoods tended to be uniformly assessed at values less than the selling price. Properties in the lower-income area had less consistent patterns, but had clearly had a number of overassessed properties.

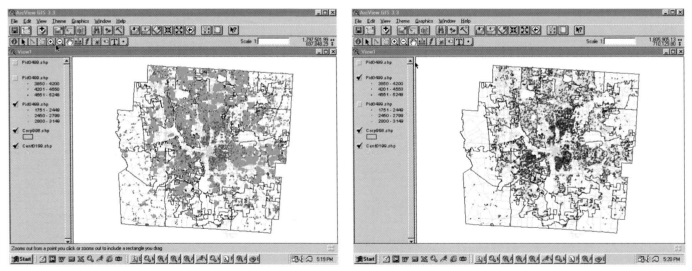

One map displayed the residential properties in Franklin County whose assessments were less than 90 percent of their sales prices as green. The reporter used the Legend Editor to shade the points based upon the degree of underassessment. He mapped the overassessed properties (where the assessed value was more than 110 percent of the sale price) in the same way, but used points shaded red.

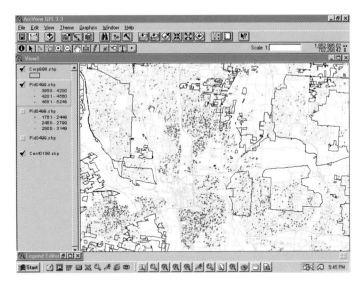

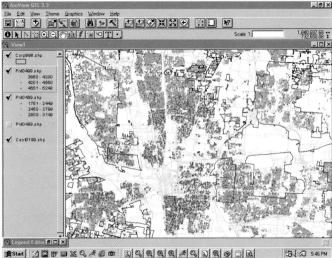

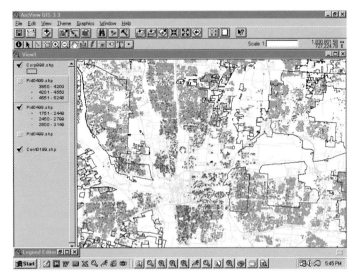

This series of ArcView images shows the assessment variations in central and east Columbus, which include low-income areas. In the first image (top left), the red points show the properties that are over-assessed. Green points in the second image (lower left) show under-assessed properties in these neighborhoods and in other residential areas. The third image (above) shows these properties together.

### Effective reporting

In its two-day series about residential assessments, the *Dispatch* reported that the homes of inner-city families were much more likely to be over-appraised than the homes of upper-income suburbanites. One-fourth of all the inner-city homeowners paid more than 110 percent of their share of the tax burden. It published two maps: one that showed the properties with high overassessments and a second that showed the properties with high underassessments.

Government officials reacted. A state representative whose district covered part of inner city Columbus said he would mail his constituents information about the assessment problems. The county auditor, an elected official, ordered his staff to review records for the parcels identified in the newspaper stories as highly over- or underassessed.

He said that the staff would send letters to home-owners with apparent incorrect assessments and suggest that they file appeals.

Later, the auditor ordered the independent appraisal firm hired by the office to investigate the assessments of four thousand residential properties whose sale values diverged widely from their assessed values. His office also sent 280,000 brochures to property owners that explained real estate taxes. The auditor later told the *Dispatch* that the mailing had prompted thirty-eight hundred additional calls from property owners.

The *Dispatch* continued to cover the increased scrutiny of the assessment process—a story that had been sparked, in part, by effective use of GIS.

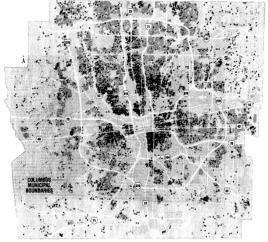

**FRANKLIN COUNTY UNDERAPPRAISED**

Used with permission of the *Columbus Dispatch*.

**FRANKLIN COUNTY OVERAPPRAISED**

Used with permission of the *Columbus Dispatch*.

The *Dispatch* ran maps with its stories about unfair assessments (also known as appraisals), including the two shown here. One map showed the properties that had been greatly underassessed (left) and the other showed the properties that had been greatly overassessed (right).

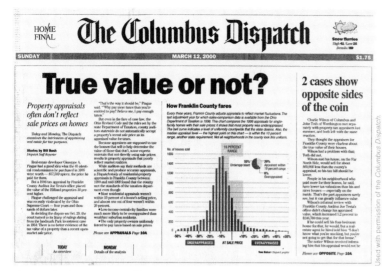

The March 12–13, 2000, editions of the *Columbus Dispatch* displayed the end result of reporting enhanced by GIS analysis: strong stories, and helpful maps showing how local government officials had unfairly assessed a number of properties to the detriment of owners.

## Acknowledgments

Bill Bush
Reporter, the *Columbus Dispatch*
For information about using GIS to report on property assessments and program screen shots.

Andy Murphy
Managing Editor, the *Columbus Dispatch*
For providing permission to reprint materials published in the *Dispatch*.

Elliot Jaspin
Systems Editor, Cox Newspapers Washington, D.C., bureau
For providing permission to use screen shot of ReelView II program.

Dan Woods
Founder, Technology Productivity Services
For providing permission to use screen shot of ReelView II program.

# 10 *Beyond traditional GIS: Using MapShop*

The case studies in this book so far have shown how journalists used traditional GIS programs in their reporting: obtaining data, mapping it, and uncovering interesting news stories. Visual journalists—the people who create the maps and graphics that help illustrate news stories—also have been using GIS. One of the tools they are using is an online service called MapShop.

MapShop is a Web-based mapping system developed by ESRI and the Associated Press. Visual journalists whose news organizations subscribe to the service can use it to create rich, accurate maps inside a browser. MapShop offers scores of map layers for the United States and the world. Though MapShop primarily is a tool for visual journalists who want to create maps for publication, it also can be used to explore geographic data and help discover newsworthy information.

Two newspapers—one large, one small—in the Great Lakes region are using MapShop to uncover information for news stories and graphics.

## Two papers

The *Chicago Tribune* and the *Times* in Munster, Indiana, sit less than thirty miles apart from each other inside the rust belt hugging Lake Michigan. The *Tribune*, whose circulation of 675,000 makes it one of the largest daily newspapers in the United States, covers the news at home and across the globe. The *Times* is much smaller, with a circulation of eighty-eight thousand. It focuses its reporting on northwest Indiana and the southeast suburbs of Chicago.

The *Tribune* has a staff of sixteen visual journalists whose maps and graphics illustrate local, state, national, and world stories in the pages of the newspaper every day. Half of those are graphics reporters who gather the information and the other half are artists who create the graphics. At the *Times,* one graphic artist makes the maps and graphics that run in the paper.

In spite of those significant differences, the two newspapers have something in common: both have used MapShop to help uncover information for stories.

Like many newspapers, the *Times* reported on the local economic, demographic, and social patterns contained in the 2000 Census data. One of the newspaper's reporters used a database manager to analyze the data for the Census stories. But when reporters for the *Times* wanted maps that showed the patterns geographically they requested them from the graphic artist, who generated them using MapShop.

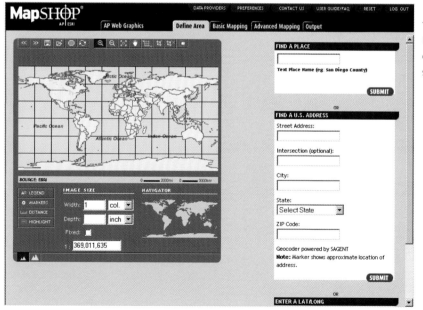

MapShop is an online GIS tool developed by ESRI and the Associated Press for use by visual journalists. MapShop contains scores of map layers that users can stitch together to create graphics or ArcView shapefiles. A MapShop demo can be accessed at *www.esri.com/mapshop.*

### Mapping racial diversity

For an early census story, a reporter wanted to locate the most racially diverse areas of Hammond, a city of eighty-three thousand near Munster, in northwest Indiana. Earlier news reports had identified Hammond as the second most diverse city in Indiana, and the reporter wanted to locate the areas inside the city that had the highest racial mix.

So the graphic artist decided to create a map that displayed the diversity—as measured by the *USA Today* Diversity Index—at the block level. The index measures the likelihood that two people picked randomly from inside an area would be of a different race. MapShop includes data from the 1990 and 2000 Census and can display patterns using different levels of geography, including blocks, block groups, and tracts. Tracts often mirror neighborhoods in urban areas.

To create the map, the graphic artist logged into MapShop. She selected Hammond, Indiana for her location. MapShop located Hammond and placed it in the center of the map window. But the map also showed the rest of the region, including Chicago and Lake Michigan, so she used the Zoom In tool to narrow the focus. Then she used the Crop tool to draw the frame for her map, and set the width to two columns to allow for greater detail.

The graphic artist at the *Times* located the city of Hammond by typing it into the Find a Place box and clicking the Submit button. MapShop users can locate places in a variety of ways.

MapShop located Hammond and centered the map on the city. It also included the surrounding region in the map window.

Then she selected U.S. Census Maps from the Base Map Layers menu. She displayed the diversity index for census block, and added highways so the reporter had a frame of reference. The map was unprojected and distorted the spatial relationships between the highways, so she clicked the Advanced Mapping tab and directed MapShop to automatically assign a projection.

Next she wanted to print the map and give a copy to the reporter. So she clicked the Output tab and selected the graphic file format she wanted—an Encapsulated PostScript (EPS) file that could be edited in a standard graphics program. She included a legend with the file so the graphic would display the diversity-index range represented by each of the colors.

Then she downloaded the file and opened it in Macromedia® FreeHand™, her graphics program. She modified the map so it would be easy to read, printed it, and gave it to the reporter who used it as a guide to find the most diverse areas of Hammond.

The graphic artist used the zoom in tool in MapShop to zero in on the city of Hammond and get to a detailed level. Then she used the U.S. Census Maps to display the diversity at the block level.

She clicked the Output tab, selected a graphics file as her output type and included a legend that displayed the diversity-index values for the colors in the blocks. In this map, darker shades of color indicate relative increases in racial diversity.

## Mapping a business story

The *Times* used MapShop again for a business news story about a shortfall of banks in low-income areas of Lake and Porter counties in Indiana, and across the border in two Illinois counties. A business reporter at the newspaper approached the graphic artist for mapping help. She wanted to plot the locations of branches listed by federal banking regulators and see whether the low-income areas had fewer.

The graphic artist logged into MapShop and it opened to the Define Area screen. She typed the street address of a branch, clicked the Submit button, and MapShop zoomed in on the address in the Basic Mapping screen and placed a marker at the location. She switched back to the Define Area screen and repeated the process to locate the other addresses. She had to download a few layers because the number of branches exceeded MapShop's limit of fifty points on one map. After creating the layers, she downloaded them in a graphics file format.

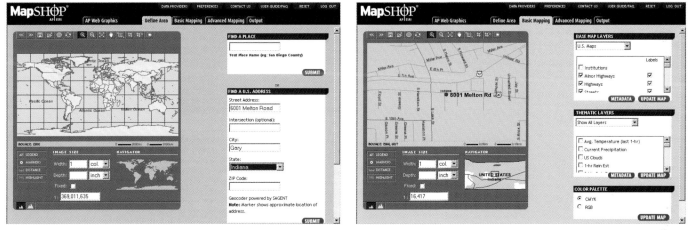

The graphic artists mapped the locations of the banks by entering their addresses in the Define Area screen.

MapShop plotted the addresses on the map and displayed the locations with a red point marker. A bank branch location is shown here.

Next she created an income map to show the median household income. With her area defined, she went to the Basic Mapping screen and selected U.S. Demographic maps, then income, and 2001 median household income for ZIP Codes. (The income forecast data came from ESRI Business Information Solutions, an affiliate of ESRI that provides demographic data to businesses.) She downloaded the map as a graphics file and then, using FreeHand, stitched it together with the point layers that she had created earlier into a graphic that showed the bank locations and the incomes of the surrounding neighborhoods.

The map showed clearly that some of the poorest areas, such as around the city of Gary, had fewer banks than wealthier suburban areas. The map ran with a story on the front page of the business section that detailed how currency exchanges, which charge higher fees for their services, outnumbered banks in the low-income areas.

The graphic artist created a map displaying median household income by ZIP Code, using 2001 data provided by ESRI Business Information Solutions (*www.esribis.com*).

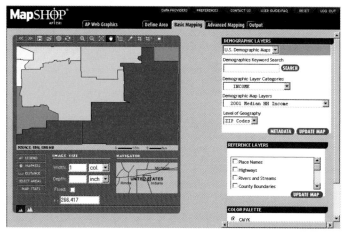

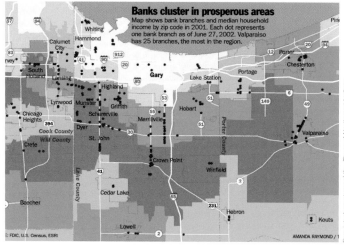

This map ran with a business news section story in the *Times* that detailed how banks favored wealthy suburban areas over the inner cities. The map showed that the banks (represented by point symbols) were more prevalent in the high-income areas (the darker shades) than the low-income areas (the lighter shades).

## Various map uses

The *Chicago Tribune* had been a MapShop test site during the development of the system, using it mostly for generating the half-dozen or so locator maps that run in the paper every day. They also used MapShop to create graphics that illustrated stories arising from the 2000 Census. The newspaper merged those two types of maps into one graphic in November 2001, when a commercial airliner exploded just after takeoff and crashed into a Queens, New York, neighborhood.

The *Tribune* wanted its map to show two things: exactly where the plane's debris had landed, and the population on the narrow strip of land flanked by the Atlantic Ocean on the south and Jamaica Bay to the north. The crash, which came two months after the September 11 terrorist attacks, killed 260 people on board and five on the ground. Though some wondered whether terrorists had struck again, U.S. air safety investigators later ruled out sabotage.

First, the artist creating the map in MapShop entered a street address to locate the Rockaway neighborhood where the fuselage, an engine, and part of another had been found. MapShop zoomed in on the location. Then the artist chose U.S. Census Maps from the Base Map Layers dropdown menu. He zoomed close until MapShop gave him the option of mapping the data by blocks. In the Advanced Mapping screen he projected the blocks and generated a shapefile that he downloaded and opened in ArcView 3.2.

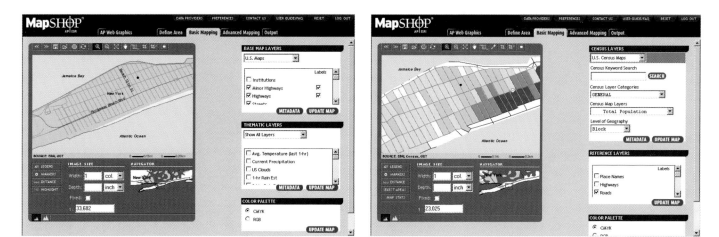

After the graphic artist entered an address in the neighborhood of the crash site, MapShop located it with a point marker.

Next the graphic artist displayed U.S. Census blocks with population data and downloaded it so he could work with it more in ArcView 3.2. In this map, darker shades of color indicate blocks with higher populations.

He tried different ways of displaying the population and settled on graduated colors that displayed the number of people in each block. The map showed that the devastation on the ground could have been much worse if the plane debris had fallen just to the southeast in the more heavily populated blocks along the ocean.

He wanted that map for part of the graphic so he used an extension to export the map as a file that he later modified in Adobe® Illustrator®, his graphics program. He returned to MapShop to create another graphics file of the area with streets and water bodies for use as a locator map. The two maps then were meshed into one graphic that ran in the newspaper the day after the crash.

The graphic that ran in the *Tribune* the day after the crash pinpointed where debris fell into the neighborhood (top map) and displayed the total population by block (bottom map).

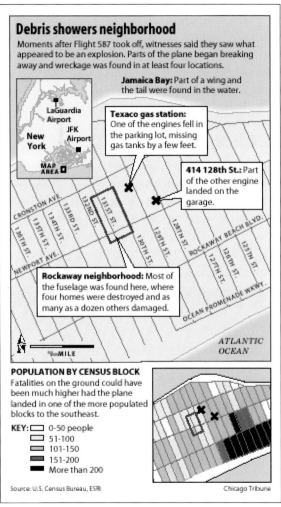

**Debris showers neighborhood**

Moments after Flight 587 took off, witnesses said they saw what appeared to be an explosion. Parts of the plane began breaking away and wreckage was found in at least four locations.

**Jamaica Bay:** Part of a wing and the tail were found in the water.

**Texaco gas station:** One of the engines fell in the parking lot, missing gas tanks by a few feet.

**414 128th St.:** Part of the other engine landed on the garage.

**Rockaway neighborhood:** Most of the fuselage was found here, where four homes were destroyed and as many as a dozen others damaged.

LaGuardia Airport
JFK Airport
New York
MAP AREA

ATLANTIC OCEAN

**POPULATION BY CENSUS BLOCK**
Fatalities on the ground could have been much higher had the plane landed in one of the more populated blocks to the southeast.

KEY: ☐ 0-50 people
☐ 51-100
▢ 101-150
▨ 151-200
■ More than 200

Source: U.S. Census Bureau, ESRI

Chicago Tribune

## Showing redistricting

The *Tribune* used MapShop again when it reported on congressional redistricting. Every ten years state legislators must redraw the boundaries of U.S. House of Representatives districts to account for population shifts reported in the decennial census.

Redistricting is a highly political process that almost always ignites allegations of favoritism. Reapportionment—or assigning the number of House seats to each state based upon population—makes the process of redistricting even more volatile when a state loses one or more of its seats.

In 2001 Illinois state lawmakers remapped the state's congressional districts. Several candidates who had campaigned hard against incumbents and planned rematches found themselves mapped into other districts. A reporter for the *Tribune* was working on a story about the redistricting and sources had told him to look closely at a few new districts.

The graphic artists at the newspaper knew that they could help tell the story visually, so one of them started working on maps that would show readers the political effects of the redistricting.

The *Tribune* already had the ArcView shapefiles for the nineteen new districts in Illinois, but the newspaper needed to get the older file with twenty districts from MapShop.

The *Tribune* already had obtained from the state legislature a shapefile with the nineteen new congressional districts. This shows the file in ArcView 3.2.

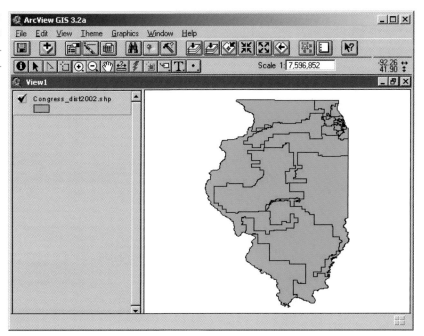

In the Basic Mapping section the artist first located the Chicago metropolitan area using the Zoom tool. Then he selected previous congressional districts and clicked Update Map to display them. He clicked the tab for the Output screen and downloaded an ArcView shapefile.

He opened the shapefile in ArcView and added a streets file. Then he geocoded the addresses of the incumbents and the recent candidates so their homes appeared as points on the map. Then he looked at the areas where the maps placed challengers into new districts. The map showed that some of the challengers found themselves just barely in new districts. The artist discovered that one was only fifty feet across the district line, another less than a block.

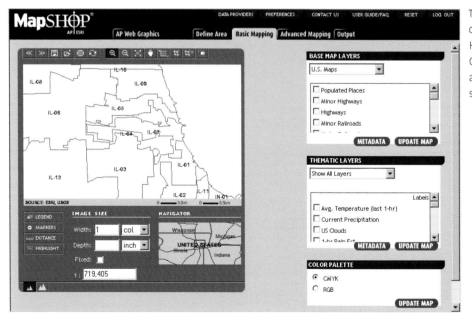

The graphic artist obtained the older congressional districts from MapShop. He used the Zoom tool to find the Chicago area, displayed the districts, and then downloaded them in a shapefile so he could use it in ArcView.

The artist exported a few of the maps from ArcView and created a graphic that showed readers how the district lines had been drawn and how the legislative remapping spared incumbents possible electoral battles against their old political rivals.

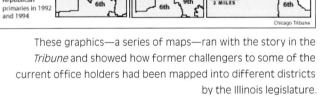

**New map shifts former opponents into new congressional district**

Three former challengers to longtime U.S. Rep. Phil Crane no longer live within the Republican's 8th District after state lawmakers approved new district boundaries in May. Other examples on **BACK PAGE**.

These graphics—a series of maps—ran with the story in the *Tribune* and showed how former challengers to some of the current office holders had been mapped into different districts by the Illinois legislature.

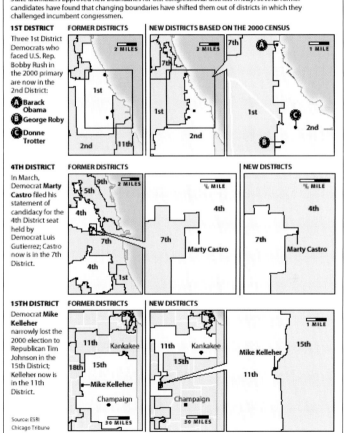

**New boundaries exclude challengers from incumbents' districts**

State lawmakers approved new boundaries for U.S. congressional districts in May. Several former candidates have found that changing boundaries have shifted them out of districts in which they challenged incumbent congressmen.

### Major series

In early 2003, the *Tribune* published "A Squandered Heritage," a three-part series about the destruction of architecturally or historically significant buildings.

MapShop helped the newspaper find destroyed buildings and show how one neighborhood had been hit hard by the demolitions. A graphics reporter downloaded recent satellite images for parts of the city from MapShop and compared them to paper copies of aerial images from past decades to find where buildings had been leveled. A satellite image of one two-block area anchored a graphic that ran with the series. Dotted lines signified the footprints of the eleven landmarks that had been destroyed from 1992 to 2000.

The series, enhanced with GIS, showed residents of Chicago how the city government failed to shield these treasured buildings. It also questioned whether a proposal by the city to place a temporary hold on building demolition permits would protect the buildings.

A *Chicago Tribune* graphic artist found a satellite image of a city neighborhood on MapShop and used it to help illustrate the demise of historically and architecturally significant buildings in a two-block area. This graphic shows eleven buildings that had been razed.

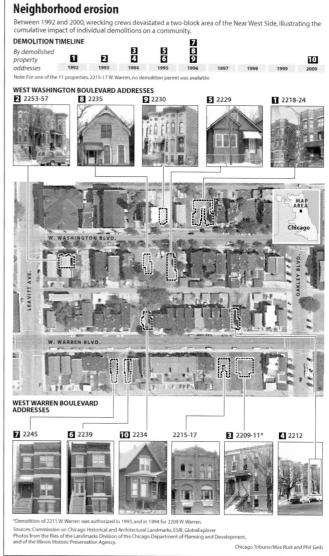

**Neighborhood erosion**

Between 1992 and 2000, wrecking crews devastated a two-block area of the Near West Side, illustrating the cumulative impact of individual demolitions on a community.

**DEMOLITION TIMELINE**

By demolished property addresses

Note: For one of the 11 properties, 2215-17 W. Warren, no demolition permit was available.

**WEST WASHINGTON BOULEVARD ADDRESSES**

2 2253-57   8 2235   9 2230   5 2229   1 2218-24

**WEST WARREN BOULEVARD ADDRESSES**

7 2245   6 2239   10 2234   2215-17   3 2209-11*   4 2212

*Demolition of 2211 W. Warren was authorized in 1993, and in 1994 for 2209 W. Warren.
Sources: Commission on Chicago Historical and Architectural Landmarks, ESRI, GlobeExplorer.
Photos from the files of the Landmarks Division of the Chicago Department of Planning and Development, and of the Illinois Historic Preservation Agency.

Chicago Tribune/Max Rust and Phil Geib

The *Chicago Tribune's* three-part "A Squandered Heritage" series ran January 13, 14, and 15, 2003, in the paper's Tempo section. The series reported in graphic detail, using maps and numerous photographs, how Chicago "failed to protect its hidden architectural gems."

**Acknowledgments**

Amanda Raymond
News Artist, *St. Petersburg Times*, formerly of the *Times* of Northwest Indiana
For providing information about using MapShop and graphics.

Pat Kincaid
Research Coordinator, the *Times* of Northwest Indiana
For providing copies of news stories.

Paul Mullaney
Managing Editor/News-Operations, the *Times* of Northwest Indiana
For providing permission to reprint newspaper graphic.

David Constantine
Associate Graphics Editor, the *Chicago Tribune*
For providing information about using MapShop and graphics.

Max Rust
Graphics Reporter, the *Chicago Tribune*
For providing information about using MapShop and graphics.

Jeannie Hoff
Information Assistant, Graphics Department, the *Chicago Tribune*
For providing newspaper copies.

Sandra Spikes
Copyright/Photosales Representative, the *Chicago Tribune*
For permission to reprint graphics.

As the case studies in this book have shown, journalists have used GIS to tell compelling news stories that mattered to readers. And the story does not end here, because the use of GIS is spreading in newsrooms story by story and graphic by graphic. The two appendixes that follow will help journalists who want to be part of that continuing story.

# A *Getting started with GIS*

More than a decade ago, the journalists who pioneered GIS as a news-reporting tool across the country faced some steep challenges. They had to master command line-programs, since many Windows-based GIS programs still were in their infancy. Second, they had to look hard to find the computer files they needed to create maps in their programs. If the map files didn't exist, then they had to create the files manually, often using paper maps as a guide. And then there was the cost: many of the GIS programs and the computers needed to run them were expensive, out of the reach of journalists working in cost-conscious newsrooms.

Plenty of newsrooms still have tight budgets, but journalists interested in GIS won't find the challenges of getting started quite as daunting. On the pages that follow are some ideas to get going, right now.

**Find a free geographic data explorer program or a public domain GIS program.**

ESRI offers ArcExplorer™ for free download at its Web site *(www.esri.com/software/arcexplorer/index.html)*. ArcExplorer is a lightweight data explorer that can display and query geographic data that's stored locally or served over the Internet. If you have a streets file with addresses, you can use the Address Matcher menu item to locate addresses.

ArcExplorer, a free program that allows you to explore and query geography data, is available for download on the ESRI Web site *(www.esri.com)*.

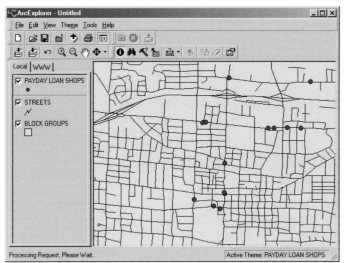

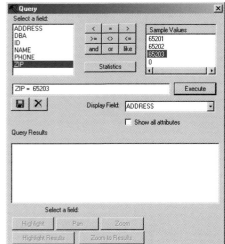

The query tool in ArcExplorer lets the user select features based upon a data attribute in the shapefile. Here, the query will select all the payday loan shop locations in the 65203 ZIP Code.

This ArcExplorer map view shows how the program displays polygon, line, and point shapefiles. The points represent the location of payday loan shops, which charge higher rates of interest than traditional banks.

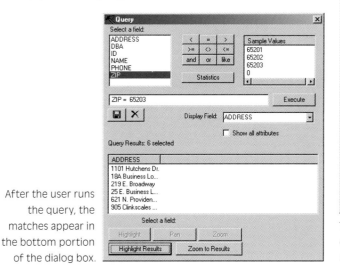

After the user runs the query, the matches appear in the bottom portion of the dialog box.

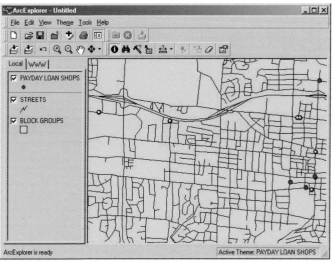

The results appear in the map view highlighted in yellow. A journalist can see exactly where the payday loan shops meeting the criteria are and can zero in on the neighborhood for his reporting.

You can also find GIS programs that are in the public domain and available at no cost. For a list of the programs and utilities, visit the Open Source GIS Web page at *www.opensourcegis.org*.

The Open Source GIS Web site: *www.opensourcegis.org*

**Start simple**

Your first story using GIS doesn't have to be an in-depth investigation that wins the Pulitzer Prize. Start simple by analyzing something basic, such as demographic patterns in your area, and producing a story. After you build expertise with the basics of GIS you can start overlaying other data to probe for interesting patterns.

Many journalists find—and some of the case studies in this book show—that GIS analysis of census data lays the groundwork for all kinds of stories. On this page are ten story ideas using data accessible to journalists.

---

**Ten GIS story ideas**

1 **Campaign financing.** Map political contributions by street address or ZIP Code. Overlay this onto a map of racial patterns, Hispanic ethnicity, or income. Report on the characteristics of the areas contributing the most money. You can then analyze the data to show where candidates draw their power.

2 **Power voters.** Plot registered voter street addresses by geocoding or mapping them by voting district. If you can get voter history data from local election authorities, go a step further and show where the most active voters live. After all, these are the people targeted by mail and door-to-door efforts during political campaigns. What are the demographic characteristics of the neighborhoods where these regular voters live? Map by party affiliation to uncover patterns.

3 **Winners and losers.** Map election results by voting district, using a dot density map. Create a density map layer with a unique symbol for each candidate and overlay these on top of census tract maps showing racial, ethnic, and income groups.

4 **Tax burdens.** Map the sale prices and assessed values of residential real estate by neighborhood or census tract to see whether any areas have a higher tax burden. Use census data to map the characteristics of the areas with higher tax burdens.

5 **Crime spots.** Get crime incident data from the police department and use geocoding to create a point map showing the locations of violent crime incidents in your city. Overlay this onto neighborhood demographic data and see whether different types of crimes plague different neighborhoods.

6 **Noisy airports.** Many major airports take regular noise readings in surrounding neighborhoods, and record the longitude and latitude where each was taken. Obtain the data and map it to show which areas suffer from the loudest airplane noise.

7 **Danger zones.** Create a point map of potentially dangerous facilities (nuclear power plants, chemical factories, and so forth) and create buffers showing the emergency planning zones. Overlay those on a population map. Show how population has grown over the past decade inside these zones.

8 **Hidden hazards.** Get a point file of leaking underground storage tank locations from your local environmental regulators and map them. Use census data to find out how many people live nearby.

9 **High-interest lenders.** Enter the addresses of payday and auto title loan locations into a data table and turn that into a point map using geocoding. Overlay the loan-shop map on demographic information to see the demographics of the neighborhoods that these shops serve.

10 **Rejected home loans.** Get the federal Home Mortgage Disclosure Act data of home loans in your area and map the rejection rates by census tract. (Make sure that you control for the income of the borrower). What are the demographics of the neighborhoods with the highest and lowest rejection rates?

### Read about GIS and mapping

There are several good books about GIS analysis and mapping that journalists can read for inspiration and education. *The ESRI Guide to GIS Analysis, Vol. 1: Geographic Patterns & Relationships* is an invaluable reference guide that focuses on how to evaluate and analyze spatial data in a variety of ways (thematic mapping, density mapping, buffering, mapping change) regardless of which GIS program you use. Many other GIS-related books are available through ESRI Press (*www.esri.com/esripress*) and other publishers.

Many journalists have found *How to Lie with Maps* by Syracuse University professor Mark Monmonier useful because it shows how maps—as supposed reflections of reality—can distort the truth. For behind-the-scenes details of GIS in news reporting, read *Uplink*, the bimonthly newsletter of the National Institute for Computer-Assisted Reporting. NICAR is a joint program of Investigative Reporters & Editors Inc., and the University of Missouri School of Journalism.

Journalists can also learn more about GIS and journalism and publishing through ESRI's media industry pages, starting at *www.esri.com/industries/media/index.html*.

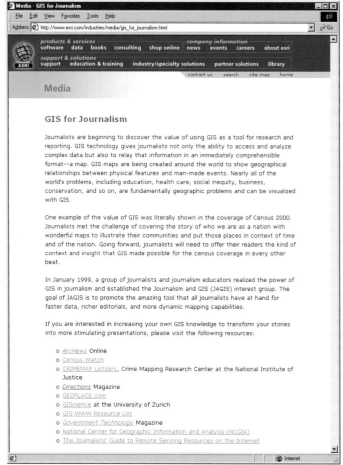

*The ESRI Guide to GIS Analysis, Vol. 1: Geographic Patterns & Relationships* provides an excellent and detailed introduction to GIS analysis for users of all GIS programs. *Uplink,* the newsletter of the National Institute for Computer-Assisted Reporting, contains regular features showing how journalists use GIS to report the news.

### Join a GIS users group

GIS users groups hold regular meetings to learn more about applying GIS to real world problems. Some users groups address GIS in general; others are designed to bring together users of specific programs. Often GIS experts will address the groups to speak about software and specific GIS projects.

### Join an e-mail list with other GIS users in journalism

Journalists using GIS share tips and tricks on these lists. Many journalists using GIS subscribe to CENSUS-L and NICAR-L, lists offered by Investigative Reporters and Editors (IRE) and the National Institute for Computer-Assisted Reporting. (For subscription information, visit *www.ire.org/ membership/listserv.html*). Many also subscribe to JAGIS-L, the journalism and GIS list run by Tom Johnson, a journalism professor at San Francisco State University. (Sign up at *groups.yahoo.com/group/ JAGIS-L.*)

### Get to know the GIS professionals in the area you cover

It pays to get acquainted with the people who are using GIS in government agencies and universities. They're often passionate about their work and love to share what they're doing with someone from the "outside world." You can also bet that they have a good handle on GIS activities in other agencies. They also will know what map data layers are available to you and may even be able to provide them at no cost. In addition, they can provide much-needed technical support if you run into any problems with the data layers.

A number of listservs are available through IRE, a grassroots, nonprofit organization formed in 1975 to improve the quality of investigative reporting and help journalists share story ideas, newsgathering techniques, and news sources.

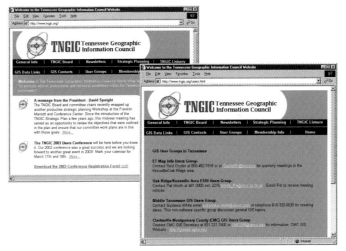

The Tennessee Geographic Information Council *(www.tngic.org)* links to a listing of Tennessee-area GIS user groups. It's one of many such entities that share GIS-related information on a broad scale.

### Know your open records laws

Obtaining GIS data—or any other electronic records for that matter—can be difficult. Journalists across the United States sometimes have to fight for access to data under their state open records laws or the federal Freedom of Information Act. Some state laws specifically make GIS data public, while other state laws fail to address electronic records at all. Amendments to some state public records laws give government agencies the authority to sell GIS data at market cost. Some states allow agencies to base the price of GIS data on the agency's geographic information system development costs. Journalists seeking data in states with amendments like those have sometimes been quoted extremely high prices for GIS data, in the thousands of dollars.

For more information about federal and state public records laws, see the Reporters Committee for Freedom of the Press Web site (*www.rcfp.org*) or the Freedom of Information Center (*foi.missouri.edu*).

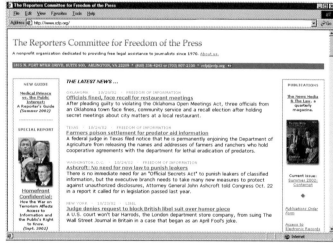

The Reporters Committee for Freedom of the Press monitors access to public records and data under state and federal laws. Its Web site contains guides to the state and federal laws.

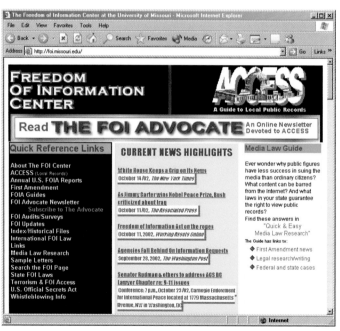

The Freedom of Information Center at the University of Missouri School of Journalism also monitors access to data and documents. Its Web site contains links that journalists requesting data may find useful.

### Read trade publications

GIS trade publications contain a wealth of information about what government agencies and GIS program developers are doing. Sometimes you can even learn about GIS projects in your own back yard. ESRI and other GIS vendors offer free newsletters and magazines about their products and user communities.

### Read consultant reports and needs assessments

Whenever a government agency establishes or expands its GIS capabilities, it first takes stock of its capabilities and outlines its needs. Sometimes agency workers themselves do this; other times a government agency hires a consultant to do the job. Regardless,

you can bet that someone will produce a GIS inventory that details the GIS hardware, software, and map layers already in use. Read these reports to learn what data is available and who holds it.

### Use free data

It's possible to use GIS in your reporting and never spend a cent on data layers. See Appendix B for free data resources.

**Department of Environmental Quality**

**Data Maintenance Responsibilities**

| Database | Coverage | Source | Scale |
|---|---|---|---|
| Non Point Source - Streams | Statewide | Oregon DEQ, Water Quality Div. | 1:250000 |
| Non-attainment Areas - Air | Statewide | Based on ODOT city boundaries | Varies |
| Volunteer Nitrate Samples | Statewide | Oregon DEQ, Water Quality Div. | PLS |
| Air Quality Emission Site | Statewide | Oregon DEQ, Admin. Systems | 1:24000 |
| Environmental Cleanup Sites | Statewide | Oregon DEQ, Admin. Systems | Tiger and Zip Center |
| Groundwater Vulnerability | Statewide | Oregon DEQ | 1:250000 |
| Sampling Stations | Statewide | Oregon DEQ via EPA's STORET | 1:100000 |
| UST and LUST Counts | Statewide | Oregon DEQ, Admin systems | Zip code and address |

**GIS Technology Investments**

Sun SparcStation with ARC/INFO, ArcView
PC with ARC/INFO, ArcView, Generic-CADD

Government agency GIS reports can be great guides for journalists who want to locate GIS layers. The reports detail the current GIS data holdings, software, and hardware. This table from a state of Oregon report shows the data layers kept by the state Department of Environmental Quality.

## Acknowledgments

Charles N. Davis
Associate Professor, University of Missouri School of Journalism and Executive
Director of the Freedom of Information Center
For providing permission to reprint Web home page graphic of the Freedom of
Information Center.

Gregg Leslie
Legal Defense Director, The Reporters Committee for Freedom of the Press
For providing permission to reprint Web page graphic of the Reporters Committee
for Freedom of the Press.

David Speight
Tennessee Geographic Information Council
For permission to reprint screen shots of the council's Web site.

Brant Houston
Executive Director, Investigative Reporters and Editors, Inc.
For permission to reprint image of the *Uplink* newsletter and permission to use the
IRE Web page graphic.

Journalists using GIS—whether they're new users or old pros—all need map layer files to display and analyze geographic information. Good map layer files are key ingredients in GIS analysis. Many journalists start with some of the fundamental map layers, such as streets, census tracts, and town boundaries. When they need other layers they add them to their collection. It's important to have accurate, up-to-date files. In areas that are growing, journalists should update parcel and subdivision files frequently. It's also good practice to frequently update streets files provided by government agencies, to ensure accuracy.

Getting GIS data for your news reporting doesn't have to break the bank. In fact, you can obtain hundreds of GIS map layers at no cost if you have a computer with an Internet connection. The following pages provide a guide to help you locate free mapping data.

## Data on CD-ROM

Most of the leading commercial GIS programs—including ArcView—come bundled with CDs containing map layers. ESRI Data & Maps contains seven CDs with layers for the world, Europe, Canada, Mexico, and the United States. Statewide layers include many of the boundaries produced by the U.S. Census Bureau (including tracts and block groups) as well as highways and waterways. Users can copy these files from CD onto a local computer or network drive for better performance.

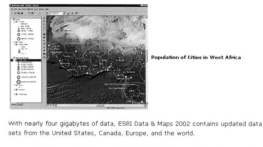

Population of Cities in West Africa

ESRI's Web pages at *www.esri.com/data/index.html* and *www.esri.com/data/datacd02.html* are among the starting points where journalists can begin to learn about acquiring valuable data.

A few federal government agencies make their GIS data available on CD–ROM at no cost. For example, the U.S. Department of Housing and Urban Development (HUD) offers its Research Maps CDs containing shapefiles and data. You can order the data online at *www.huduser.org/datasets/gis.html*. The National Transportation Atlas, as well as the North American Transportation Atlas, can be ordered from the U.S. Department of Transportation's Bureau of Transportation Statistics on the Web at *www.bts.gov/gis/ntatlas*.

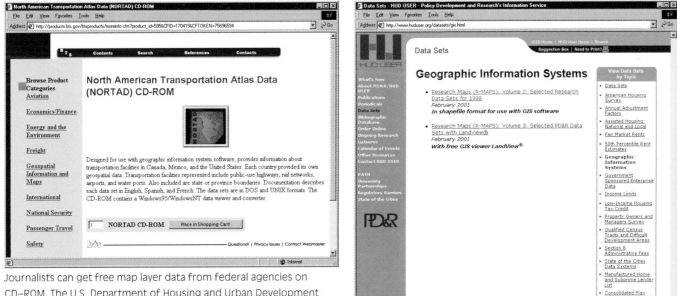

Journalists can get free map layer data from federal agencies on CD–ROM. The U.S. Department of Housing and Urban Development and the U.S. Department of Transportation both provide data in this form.

### Census files on the Internet

Many journalists find census data and map files essential in their GIS reporting. The U.S. Census Bureau Web site *(www.census.gov)* is the place to go for the source files. The Census Bureau posts its GIS files on the Web at *www.census.gov/geo/www/tiger/ index.html.* This is where you can find streets files that you'll need to geocode street address lists. The files from 1990 and 2000 are in the bureau's TIGER mapping system format, but you can easily convert them to GIS program file formats using third-party utility programs.

The U.S. Census Bureau Web site hosts a wealth of map layer and attribute data that journalists can use in their reporting. The bureau's TIGER geography page contains map layer data that GIS users can convert and use in their programs.

If you don't care to convert the data yourself, you can download map shapefiles from the 2000 Census from the ESRI Web site *(arcdata.esri.com/data/ tiger2000/tiger_download.cfm)* at no cost. You can also download Census demographic data files from this site that can be joined to the shapefiles in ArcView.

Need earlier mapping layers for census boundaries? The Center for International Earth Science Information Network (CIESIN) Archive of Census-related GIS products *(www.ciesin.org)* is a good place to start looking.

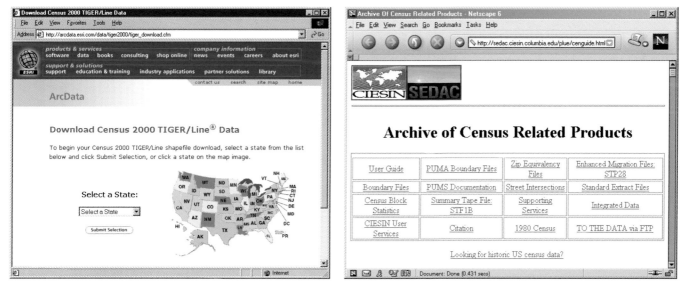

ESRI makes census shapefiles available on its Web site for free download. Journalists also can find older census mapping files at the CIESIN data archive.

**The Geography Network**

ESRI's Geography Network℠ *(www.geographynetwork.com)* provides access to free and commercial data from government agencies and vendors that journalists can use for their reporting projects. Journalists can obtain flood-zone boundary files, elevation layers, and aerial photography that's been prepared for use with ArcView.

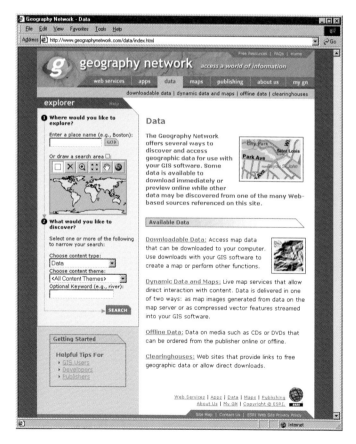

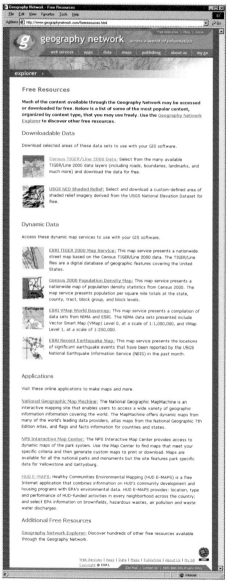

The Geography Network is a global network of geographic information users and providers. Through it, journalists can access many types of geographic content including dynamic maps, downloadable data, and more advanced Web services.

## Uncle Sam's offerings

The federal government offers much more than Census map layers. Almost every federal agency, it seems, posts some map layers on the Web. It's difficult to keep track of everything that's available, but a good starting point is the National Geospatial Data Clearinghouse *(130.11.52.184)*. The clearinghouse is the U.S. government's attempt to index and organize GIS data, from the local to international level.

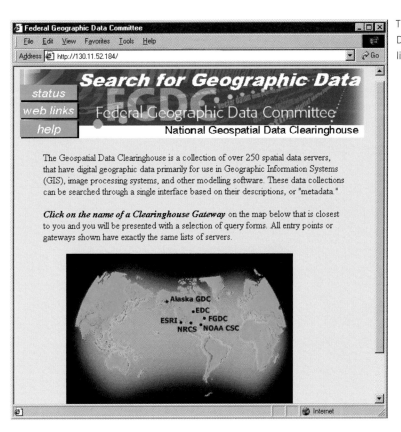

The National Geospatial Data Clearinghouse has links to GIS search tools.

The U.S. Geological Survey *(www.usgs.gov)* is the federal government's chief civilian mapping operation and makes many of its GIS products available for free on the Internet. Start by checking out the National Mapping Information site *(mapping.usgs.gov)*.

The U.S. Geological Survey is the country's primary civilian mapping service. Its Web page is a good place to start looking for GIS data. The agency also maintains the National Mapping Information Web page and the Earth Resources Observation System (EROS) Data Center.

The U.S. Geological Survey makes its image data—called raster data—available on a number of its Web sites. The image data includes topographic maps and satellite photos that can be imported into a GIS program. Some of the imagery can be used to show land elevation and use, and changes in environmental conditions. The Earth Resources Observation Systems (EROS) Data Center *(edc.usgs.gov)* is a good place to start searching. Microsoft makes some of the same imagery available on its Terraserver at *www.terraserver.microsoft.com.*

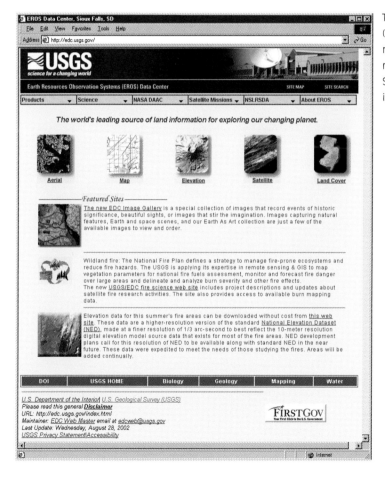

The Earth Resources Observation Systems (EROS) Data Center (EDC) is a data management, systems development, and research field center for the U.S. Geological Survey's National Mapping Division. The EDC is based near Sioux Falls, South Dakota.

Some federal agencies strive to put their GIS data on one Web page. The U.S. Environmental Protection Agency's EnviroMapper Storefront is a good example *(www.epa.gov/enviro/html/em)* of a centralized agency site.

Finding map layers can be an overwhelming task. Try using an Internet search site to find files with the *.shp* or *.E00* extension on federal government Web sites (having the *.gov* domain). You can try a similar strategy to find map layers on state government, nonprofit *(.org),* and educational institution *(.edu)* sites.

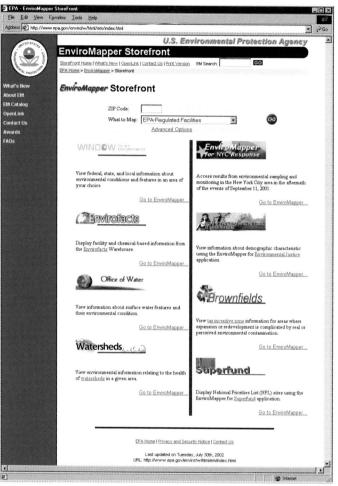

The U.S. Environmental Protection Agency makes its GIS data available at one spot on the Internet, the EnviroMapper Storefront.

## Locating state data

Almost every state has started compiling GIS data in one location and making it available on the Web. Rhode Island *(www.edc.uri.edu/rigis)* and Delaware *(www.datamil.udel.edu/nationalmappilot)* both allow users to download shapefiles of dozens of data sets. If you're looking for data in your state, you can start with the data clearinghouse list compiled by the University of Arkansas at *www.cast.uark.edu/local/hunt*.

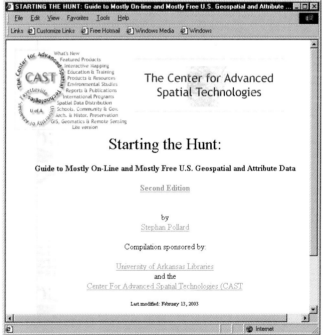

The Center for Advanced Spatial Technologies, based at the University of Arkansas at Fayetteville, maintains a list of state GIS clearinghouse Web sites

Journalists can find map layer files on the state of Delaware's DataMIL Web site. Using the Extract function, users can download the map layer files and open them in ArcView.

## Acknowledgments

Stephen Pollard
Environmental Dynamics Ph.D. Program
For providing permission to reprint the Center for Advanced Spatial Technologies
"Starting the Hunt" Web page.

# *Other books from* **ESRI Press**

## *GIScience*

The ESRI Guide to GIS Analysis, Volume 1: Geographic Patterns and Relationships
An important book about how to do real analysis with a geographic information system. *The ESRI Guide to GIS Analysis* focuses on six of the most common geographic analysis tasks.
ISBN 1-879102-06-4  188 pages

Modeling Our World: The ESRI Guide to Geodatabase Design
With this comprehensive guide and reference to GIS data modeling and to the new geodatabase model introduced with ArcInfo™ 8, you will learn how to make the right decisions about modeling data, from database design and data capture to spatial analysis and visual presentation.
ISBN 1-879102-62-5  216 pages

Hydrologic and Hydraulic Modeling Support with Geographic Information Systems
This book presents the invited papers in water resources at the 1999 ESRI® International User Conference. Covering practical issues related to hydrologic and hydraulic water quantity modeling support using GIS, the concepts and techniques apply to any hydrologic and hydraulic model requiring spatial data or spatial visualization.  ISBN 1-879102-80-3  232 pages

Beyond Maps: GIS and Decision Making in Local Government
*Beyond Maps* shows how local governments are making geographic information systems true management tools. Packed with real-life examples, it explores innovative ways to use GIS to improve local government operations.  ISBN 1-879102-79-X  240 pages

The ESRI Press Dictionary of GIS Terminology
This long-needed and authoritative reference brings together the language and nomenclature of the many GIS-related disciplines and applications. Designed for students, professionals, researchers, and technicians, the dictionary provides succinct and accurate definitions of more than a thousand terms.
ISBN 1-879102-78-1  128 pages

Planning Support Systems: Integrating Geographic Information Systems, Models, and Visualization Tools
Richard Brail of Rutgers University's Edward J. Bloustein School of Planning and Public Policy, and Richard Klosterman of the University of Akron, have assembled papers from colleagues around the globe who are working to expand the applicability and understanding of the top issues in computer-aided planning.
ISBN 1-58948-011-2  468 pages

Geographic Information Systems and Science
This comprehensive guide to GIS, geographic information science (GIScience), and GIS management illuminates some shared concerns of business, government, and science. It looks at how issues of management, ethics, risk, and technology intersect, and at how GIS provides a gateway to problem solving, and links to special learning modules at ESRI Virtual Campus (campus.esri.com).
ISBN 0-471-89275-0  472 pages

Undersea with GIS
Explore how GIS is illuminating the mysteries hidden in the earth's oceans. Applications include managing protected underwater sanctuaries, tracking whale migration, and recent advances in 3-D electronic navigation. The companion CD brings the underwater world to life for both the undersea practitioner and student and includes 3-D underwater fly-throughs, ArcView® extensions for marine applications, a K–12 lesson plan, and more.  ISBN 1-58948-016-3  276 pages

Past Time, Past Place: GIS for History
In this pioneering book that encompasses the Greek and Roman eras, the Salem witch trials, the Dust Bowl of the 1930s, and much more, leading scholars explain how GIS technology can illuminate the study of history. Richly illustrated, *Past Time, Past Place* is a vivid supplement to many courses in cultural studies and will fascinate armchair historians.  ISBN 1-58948-032-5  224 pages

Arc Hydro: GIS for Water Resources
Based on ESRI ArcGIS® software, the Arc Hydro data model provides a new and standardized way of describing hydrologic data to consistently and efficiently solve water resource problems at any spatial scale. This book is a blueprint of the model and the definitive overview of GIS in hydrology from the field's leading expert. The companion CD includes Arc Hydro instructions, tools, teacher resources, and data.  ISBN 1-58948-034-1  220 pages

Confronting Catastrophe: A GIS Handbook
This hands-on manual is for GIS practitioners and decision makers whose communities face the threat of large-scale disasters, whether they be wildfires, hurricanes, earthquakes, or now, terrorist attacks. Real-world lessons show public officials and IT managers how to use GIS most efficiently in the five stages of disaster management: identification and planning, mitigation, preparedness, response, and recovery.  ISBN 1-58948-040-6  156 pages

A System for Survival: GIS and Sustainable Development
The goal of sustainable development is to raise standards of living worldwide without depleting resources or destroying habitat. This book provides examples of how geographic technologies, by synthesizing the vast amounts of data being collected about natural resources, population, health, public safety, and more, can play a creative and constructive role in the realization of that goal.
ISBN 1-58948-052-X  124 pages

Marine Geography: GIS for the Oceans and Seas
This collection of case studies documents some of the many current applications of marine GIS. The contributing authors share their work, challenges, successes, and progress in the use of GIS, and show how the technology is being used to influence the decision-making process in a way that leads to healthy and sustainable oceans and seas.  ISBN 1-58948-045-7  228 pages

*CONTINUED ON NEXT PAGE*

# Other books from **ESRI Press** *continued*

## *The Case Studies Series*

### ArcView GIS Means Business
Written for business professionals, this book is a behind-the-scenes look at how some of America's most successful companies have used desktop GIS technology. The book is loaded with full-color illustrations and comes with a trial copy of ArcView software and a GIS tutorial. ISBN 1-879102-51-X 136 pages

### Zeroing In: Geographic Information Systems at Work in the Community
In twelve "tales from the digital map age," this book shows how people use GIS in their daily jobs. An accessible and engaging introduction to GIS for anyone who deals with geographic information. ISBN 1-879102-50-1 128 pages

### Serving Maps on the Internet
Take an insider's look at how today's forward-thinking organizations distribute map-based information via the Internet. Case studies cover a range of applications for ArcView Internet Map Server technology from ESRI. This book should interest anyone who wants to publish geospatial data on the Web. ISBN 1-879102-52-8 144 pages

### Managing Natural Resources with GIS
Find out how GIS technology helps people design solutions to such pressing challenges as wildfires, urban blight, air and water degradation, species endangerment, disaster mitigation, coastline erosion, and public education. The experiences of public and private organizations provide real-world examples. ISBN 1-879102-53-6 132 pages

### Enterprise GIS for Energy Companies
A volume of case studies showing how electric and gas utilities use geographic information systems to manage their facilities more cost effectively, find new market opportunities, and better serve their customers. ISBN 1-879102-48-X 120 pages

### Transportation GIS
From monitoring rail systems and airplane noise levels, to making bus routes more efficient and improving roads, the twelve case studies in this book show how geographic information systems have emerged as the tool of choice for transportation planners. ISBN 1-879102-47-1 132 pages

### GIS for Landscape Architects
From Karen Hanna, noted landscape architect and GIS pioneer, comes *GIS for Landscape Architects*. Through actual examples, you will learn how landscape architects, land planners, and designers now rely on GIS to create visual frameworks within which spatial data and information are gathered, interpreted, manipulated, and shared. ISBN 1-879102-64-1 120 pages

### GIS for Health Organizations
Health management is a rapidly developing field, where even slight shifts in policy affect the health care we receive. In this book, you will see how physicians, public health officials, insurance providers, hospitals, epidemiologists, researchers, and HMO executives use GIS to focus resources to meet the needs of those in their care. ISBN 1-879102-65-X 112 pages

### GIS in Public Policy: Using Geographic Information for More Effective Government
This book shows how policy makers and others on the front lines of public service are putting GIS to work—to carry out the will of voters and legislators, and to inform and influence their decisions. *GIS in Public Policy* shows vividly the very real benefits of this new digital tool for anyone with an interest in, or influence over, the ways our institutions shape our lives. ISBN 1-879102-66-8 120 pages

### Integrating GIS and the Global Positioning System
The Global Positioning System is an explosively growing technology. *Integrating GIS and the Global Positioning System* covers the basics of GPS and presents several case studies that illustrate some of the ways the power of GPS is being harnessed to GIS, ensuring, among other benefits, increased accuracy in measurement and completeness of coverage. ISBN 1-879102-81-1 112 pages

### GIS in Schools
GIS is transforming classrooms—and learning—in elementary, middle, and high schools across North America. *GIS in Schools* documents what happens when students are exposed to GIS. The book gives teachers practical ideas about how to implement GIS in the classroom, and some theory behind the success stories. ISBN 1-879102-85-4 128 pages

### Disaster Response: GIS for Public Safety
GIS is making emergency management faster and more accurate in responding to natural disasters, providing a comprehensive and effective system of preparedness, mitigation, response, and recovery. Case studies describe GIS use in siting fire stations, routing emergency response vehicles, controlling wildfires, assisting earthquake victims, improving public disaster preparedness, and much more. ISBN 1-879102-88-9 124 pages

### Open Access: GIS in e-Government
A revolution taking place on the Web is transforming the traditional relationship between government and citizens. At the forefront of this e-government revolution are agencies using GIS to serve interactive maps over their Web sites and, in the process, empower citizens. This book presents case studies of a cross-section of these forward-thinking agencies. ISBN 1-879102-87-0 124 pages

### GIS in Telecommunications
Global competition is forcing telecommunications companies to stretch their boundaries as never before—requiring efficiency and innovation in every aspect of the enterprise if they are to survive, prosper, and come out on top. The ten case studies in this book detail how telecommunications competitors worldwide are turning to GIS to give them the edge they need. ISBN 1-879102-86-2 120 pages

### Conservation Geography: Case Studies in GIS, Computer Mapping, and Activism
This collection of dozens of case studies tells of the ways GIS is revolutionizing the work of nonprofit organizations and conservation groups worldwide as they rush to save the earth's plants, animals, and cultural and natural resources. As these pages show clearly, the power of computers and GIS is transforming the way environmental problems and conservation issues are identified, measured, and ultimately, resolved. ISBN 1-58948-024-4 252 pages

### GIS Means Business, Volume Two
For both business professionals and general readers, *GIS Means Business, Volume Two* presents more companies and organizations, including a chamber of commerce, a credit union, colleges, reinsurance and real estate firms, and more, who have used ESRI software to become more successful. See how businesses use GIS to solve problems, make smarter decisions, enhance customer service, and discover new markets and profit opportunities. ISBN 1-58948-033-3 188 pages

## ESRI Software Workbooks

Understanding GIS: The ARC/INFO® Method (Version 7.2 for UNIX® and Windows NT®)
A hands-on introduction to GIS technology. Designed primarily for beginners, this classic text guides readers through a complete GIS project in ten easy-to-follow lessons. ISBN 1-879102-01-3  608 pages

ARC Macro Language: Developing ARC/INFO Menus and Macros with AML
ARC Macro Language (AML™) software gives you the power to tailor workstation ARC/INFO software's geoprocessing operations to specific applications. This workbook teaches AML in the context of accomplishing practical workstation ARC/INFO tasks, and presents both basic and advanced techniques. ISBN 1-879102-18-8  828 pages

Getting to Know ArcView GIS
A colorful, nontechnical introduction to GIS technology and ArcView software, this best-selling workbook comes with a working ArcView demonstration copy. Follow the book's scenario-based exercises or work through them using the CD and learn how to do your own ArcView project. ISBN 1-879102-46-3  660 pages

Extending ArcView GIS
This sequel to the award-winning Getting to Know ArcView GIS is written for those who understand basic GIS concepts and are ready to extend the analytical power of the core ArcView software. The book consists of short conceptual overviews followed by detailed exercises framed in the context of real problems. ISBN 1-879102-05-6  540 pages

GIS for Everyone, Third Edition
This self-study workbook will have anyone—student, small business owner, or community leader—creating GIS projects within minutes. Using data from the CD and from the Geography Network™, readers can create digital maps and simple geographic analyses for school, work, or Web. The revised third edition of this all-time GIS bestseller includes ArcExplorer™ 2 and ArcExplorer 4 Java™ Edition GIS software and more than 500 megabytes of geographic data. ISBN 1-58948-056-2  160 pages

Getting to Know ArcGIS Desktop: Basics of ArcView, ArcEditor™, and ArcInfo
Getting to Know ArcGIS Desktop is a workbook for learning ArcGIS, the newest GIS technology from ESRI. Learn to use the building blocks of ArcGIS: ArcMap™, for displaying and querying maps; ArcCatalog™, for managing geographic data; and ArcToolbox™, for setting map projections and converting data. Illustrations and exercises teach basic GIS tasks. Includes a 180-day trial version of ArcView 8 software on CD and a CD of data for working through the exercises. ISBN 1-879102-89-7  552 pages

Mapping Our World: GIS Lessons for Educators
A comprehensive educational resource that gives any teacher all the tools needed to begin teaching GIS technology in the middle- or high-school classroom. Includes nineteen complete GIS lesson plans, a one-year license of ArcView 3.x, geographic data, a teacher resource CD, and a companion Web site. ISBN 1-58948-022-8  564 pages

Community Geography: GIS in Action
Seven innovative case studies and accompanying exercises will inspire students, teachers, and active citizens to use GIS to tackle problems in their own communities. The step-by-step exercises incorporate spatial thinking, GIS software, the geographic inquiry method, and real data from the case studies. Includes data CD (Microsoft® Windows®- and Apple® Macintosh®-compatible). ISBN 1-58948-023-6  296 pages

Community Geography: GIS in Action Teacher's Guide
Written by teachers for teachers, this companion to Community Geography: GIS in Action provides tips, resources, and guidance to teachers undertaking GIS projects with students. Anticipates needs, issues, and questions and includes middle- and high-school companion lesson plans for use with the exercises and projects in Community Geography: GIS in Action. ISBN 1-58948-051-1  152 pages

## Atlases

Mapping Census 2000: The Geography of U.S. Diversity
Cartographers Cynthia A. Brewer and Trudy A. Suchan have taken Census 2000 data and assembled an atlas of maps that illustrates the new American diversity in rich and vivid detail. The result is an atlas of America and of Americans that is notable both for its comprehensiveness and for its precision. ISBN 1-58948-014-7  120 pages

Salton Sea Atlas
Explore the scientific, historical, and physical dimensions of California's unique Salton Sea region, a nexus of the forces of nature and the momentum of human civilization, in the pages of this groundbreaking benchmark reference. Cutting-edge GIS technology was used to transform vast amounts of data into multilayered, multithemed maps as visually compelling as they are revelatory. ISBN 1-58948-043-0  136 pages

ESRI Map Book, Volume 17: Geography and GIS—Sustaining Our World
A full-color collection of some of the finest maps produced using GIS software. Published annually since 1984, this unique book celebrates the mapping achievements of GIS professionals. Directions Magazine (www.directionsmag.com) has called the ESRI Map Book "The best map book in print." ISBN 1-58948-048-1  120 pages

*ESRI educational products cover topics related to geographic information science, GIS applications, and ESRI technology. You can choose among instructor-led courses, Web-based courses, and self-study workbooks to find education solutions that fit your learning style and pocketbook. Visit www.esri.com/education for more information.*

*ESRI Press publishes a growing list of GIS-related books. Ask for these books at your local bookstore or order by calling 1-800-447-9778. You can also shop online at www.esri.com/gisstore. Outside the United States, contact your local ESRI distributor.*

ESRI Press • 380 New York Street • Redlands, California 92373-8100 • www.esri.com/esripress

*Mapping the News: Case Studies in GIS and Journalism*
Book design, production, and image editing by Jennifer Galloway
Cover design by Denise Marshall
Copyediting by Tiffany Wilkerson
Printing coordination by Cliff Crabbe